This is a story of creating extraordinary results. Silverado Senior Living is about living to our fullest, knowing "and" is more powerful than "or" -- just as love is more powerful than fear. Any leader exploring how his or her organization can achieve more will find this easy-to-read story of innovation, courage and conviction to be inspiring and useful.

Vance Caesar, Ph.D.

This book describes the philosophy and heart of the Silverado approach. The organization has developed a model for the care of the cognitively impaired that is being copied worldwide. It balances the needs for safety and independence in a way that is difficult to understand unless you see it yourself. The concept of community at Silverado is well described in this book and so are the motivations and approaches utilized by its leadership in the entire organization. This book is very useful reading for families of people with Alzheimer's and other dementias and for everyone caring for them.

Joe W. Ramsdell, M.D., Division Head, General Internal Medicine;
Professor of Clinical Medicine; Professor of Pulmonary; Director,
Clinical Trials Center, University of California, San Diego

Magicians rarely reveal the secrets of their 'tricks', fearing we will lose our enthusiasm for what they have done. Some people's endeavors seem 'magical' to onlookers, who see them doing things that seemed impossible. In the past 10 years I've had many occasions to watch the 'magic' of Silverado's residential communities, home care services, and hospice services. Each time I'm amazed at the results but I've always known they were from beliefs and actions that any of us can grasp and practice. In this volume, the secrets are revealed and it will hopefully bring others to demand and to create the same quality of thought and care for people with memory-impairing disease. The book offers guidance to both the mindset and the programs that will change their futures — and ours.

Cathy Greenblat, Ph.D., sociologist, photographer,
author of "Alive With Alzheimer's" and the forthcoming
"Love, Loss And Laughter: Seeing Alzheimer's Differently"

"Inspiring" is a word too lightly used today. Finding that internal spark and having it blossom into an inferno of creativity and passion - all lit by someone else's fire - is a rare happening. Loren Shook and the Silverado team have truly inspired thousands to see that one's humanity does not diminish with the onset of dementia. His vision and willingness to exchange fear for love has ignited a fire of compassion, care and commitment that extends far beyond the walls of Silverado. His story and the story of an amazing company, as well as the daily example they set for all of us, change lives every day – with love.

Jim McAleer, President & CEO, Alzheimer's Association
–Orange County, Calif. Chapter

The contribution and vision Loren Shook has gifted to Silverado and its culture of caring for seniors challenged with memory-impairing conditions is nothing short of extraordinary. Being a corporate executive and speaking a language outside of cash flow, pre-tax, EBIDA, and margins takes courage, foresight and risk. His trueness to self and truly understanding the dignity to serve this patient population, these families, and community of concern at large has changed the face of providing care in this specialty. Being a change agent and a rebel of thought requires a certain type of person with a unique vision. What a blessing to have a person like Loren to teach all of us the depth of meaning of such a small but powerful word that launched ships and founded nations: love!

Peter F. Bastone, President & CEO,
Mission Hospital, Mission Viejo and Laguna Beach, Calif.

"The Silverado Story" is a moving, life-affirming, and thought-provoking reflection on how the world can provide outstanding care for people with Alzheimer's disease and other forms of memory loss. This book will enlighten and inspire policy makers, regulators, providers, family members and others who have responsibility for the care of seniors with this devastating disease.

Richard P. Grimes, President & CEO, Assisted Living Federation of America

"Reaching and nurturing the human spirit…"

"Lives lived with passion and purpose…"

"Satisfying the need to be understood…"

Perhaps they are not the kind of statements you might expect to be associated with caring for the memory impaired, but they capture what "The Silverado Story" is all about. Beginning with the personal story of Loren Shook and continuing with countless tales of caregivers, the children of caregivers, volunteers – and, most importantly, the residents themselves – this book will inspire readers by reminding them what truly moves each of us as human beings and, in so doing, it will profoundly change their understanding of the memory impaired.

Robert G. Kramer, President,
National Investment Center for the Seniors Housing & Care Industry

"The Silverado Story: A Memory Care-Culture Where Love is Greater Than Fear" should be mandatory reading for everyone in the assisted living and long-term care profession. Loren Shook and Steve Winner share their winning vision in a well-written, passionate and inspirational book with insights that resonate deeply on both the personal and professional levels.

David S. Schless, President, American Seniors Housing Association

"The Silverado Story" leaves no doubt that love and compassion comprise the greatest means of touching the human spirit. Loren Shook and Steve Winner give a powerful testimony to the healing value of compassion and love, sharing touching examples of how lives are changed when fear is replaced by love in our everyday living.

W.E. (Bill) Sheriff, CEO, Brookdale Senior Living

A passion for quality of life, dignity, and love above all else – that is Loren Shook and Silverado.

Granger Cobb, President & Co-CEO, Emeritus Senior Living

Is it possible to successfully operate a company based on the principle that "Love is greater than fear?" Loren Shook and Steve Winner are proving this motto can be the lodestar for an organization dedicated to making the world a better place for those with memory impairment.

Their story is a testimony to the truth that values and positive attitudes do make a difference in the success of a business – both for the owners and the clients.

Lives never lose meaning at Silverado. Residents can still contribute through the Silverado Service Club – volunteering time and talent to help others in the greater community. The continual presence of children and animals helps those slipping from reality remain empowered.

I've been writing about aging issues – including dementias – for almost two decades. Much of my reporting has focused on the unhappiness of people confined to care environments. What a pleasure to know there are those who genuinely care about these residents and that there are communities filled with sunlight and love.

Jane Glenn Haas, journalist, speaker and author, "Time of Your Life"

People with dementia have so much to offer and they are here to teach us what is important in life. Not what day it is or what we had for lunch, but what it means to reach a human soul. When we glimpse their soul, we have had a glimpse of our own. This book has captured the essence of the soul and of LOVE in all of us.

Jolene Brackey, speaker and author, "Creating Moments of Joy"

I read "The Silverado Story" with more than just casual interest. I have lived "The Silverado Story." My beloved mother spent the last five years of her life at a Silverado community. I visited my mother nearly every day and saw the way in which Silverado took care of not just my mother, but all residents of her community. A different kind of care is provided -- care a person will not find anywhere else. The stimulation residents receive; the respect they are shown by the staff; the love that is evident makes each visit to Silverado a special one. I loved my mother and I would not wish this disease on anyone. However, Silverado provided her, and just as importantly, our family, an environment during her final years that was worthy of her. It could not have been better.

Patrick C. Haden

Having been deeply entrenched in the world of caregiving for family members for over 15 years, I'm deeply touched by "The Silverado Story" and by the work being done by Silverado Senior Living. Helping the world understand that the human spirit remains even when it can't always be expressed by the memory impaired is a lofty goal. The "Silverado Story" has convinced me, and I believe this story will change the world's view of people with memory impairment as well. If my memory fails me at some point, Silverado is where I want to be.

Karen L. Twichell, Author/Speaker,
"A Caregiver's Journey ~ Finding Your Way," www.caregiversjourney.com

When my mother was diagnosed with Alzheimer's disease in her late seventies, it was a familiar situation. My father had died from complications with Alzheimer's a few years earlier. At this time, I was her primary caregiver, and one of the most painful aspects, among many, was her constant search for a purpose, a reason to go on. She kept saying, "I need a job." Of course, this was an impossibility and yet every time I could come up with a task for her to accomplish, her entire demeanor changed. She became energized, bright, and engaged.

I felt that a program must be developed in communities dealing with dementia that would enable residents to feel motivated and purposeful. In "The Silverado Story," Loren Shook and Steve Winner identify an ideology that encompasses this concern and so many others. I am hopeful that this innovative book will impact senior care organizations everywhere.

Victor Garber, film, television and stage actor

THE SILVERADO STORY

A MEMORY-CARE CULTURE WHERE LOVE IS GREATER THAN FEAR

LOREN SHOOK AND STEPHEN WINNER

AJC Press
6400 Oak Canyon, Suite #200
Irvine, California 92618
www.silveradostory.com

ISBN: 978-0-9845337-5-6
LCCN: 2010912425

Publisher's Cataloging-in-Publication Data

Shook, Loren.

The Silverado story : a memory-care culture where love is greater than fear / Loren Shook and Stephen Winner. -- 1st ed. -- Irvine, CA : AJC Press, c2010.

p. ; cm.

ISBN: 978-0-9845337-5-6

1. Alzheimer's disease--Alternative treatment. 2. Alzheimer's disease--Patients--Rehabilitation. 3. Memory disorders--Alternative treatment. 4. Memory disorders--Patients--Rehabilitation. 5. Silverado Senior Living--History. I. Winner, Stephen. II. Silverado Senior Living. III. Title.

RC523.2 .S46 2010   2010912425
361.1/96831--dc22   1010

Dust jacket and book design: Sean Glumace
Cover Photography: Lia Segerblom, Lia Photography

This book is intended for your enjoyment and general education only. This is not an authoritative medical manual, though this publication is designed to provide accurate and important information regarding the subject matter. Everyone is a unique individual with their own specific medical history and needs, so if professional medical advice or other expert assistance is required regarding any of the matters covered in this book, the services of a professional should be sought.

Printed in the United States of America.

DEDICATIONS

From Loren

To my father and mother, **Cleo and Kathleen Shook**, who taught me the meaning of love, responsibility, a work ethic and values, and introduced me to the power of God, the spirit that lives within all of us.

To my aunt and uncle, **Bernard and Marion Hambleton**, who showed me how to combine innovation and ingenuity with the best physicians to create and operate a state of the art psychiatric hospital including specialized service for people with any type of memory-impairing disease.

To my children, **Heather**, **Aaron**, **Christine**, **John-Colby** and **Arianna**, each of whom is a part of my reason for being.

To my loving wife, **Suzanne**, who is always there for me – my greatest cheerleader, confidant and best friend.

From Steve

To **Dr. Wolf Wolfensberger** who showed me the intrinsic values in everyone.

To **Kennon S. Shea** who gave me the freedom and encouragement to be creative.

To **Richard Mendlen** who taught me how to lead others with love and strength.

DEDICATIONS

From Steve (Continued)

To **Jack Peters** who has supported me and Silverado every day with his knowledge, experience, keen insight and sense of humor.

To **Loren Shook**, my friend, mentor and inspirational leader, who found me in a niche and opened up the world.

To my daughter, **Elizabeth**, who filled a void in my life so deep I didn't know it was there.

To my wife, **Deanelle**, who stood with me through good times and bad and who fearlessly stood beside me as we rolled the dice to follow my dreams.

From Loren and Steve

To the memory of our co-founder, **Jim Smith**, whose courageous investment of time, money and expertise together with his extraordinary sense of humor were invaluable in creating Silverado as it is today.

We could not have built the company without the effort and support of **Jim and his wife, Nancy**.

Contents

Foreword

If I had parents with Alzheimer's disease, I would want them to live at Silverado.

If I had a spouse with memory impairment, I would want him to spend his days at Silverado.

If I had a teenager needing to perform community service, I would want her to do it at Silverado.

If I had a puppy in need of a home, I would want that home to be Silverado.

In more than three decades of living and working with cognitively-impaired adults, I have not felt so compelled to see a story told as in "The Silverado Story," by its principals Loren Shook and Stephen Winner.

What Silverado knows is that the human spirit glows until we take our last breath … Memory impairment does not mean the spirit is not present. It still shines but speaks differently.

Whether it is through their collaboration as an active research site with leading medical schools, their commitment to taking care of those caring for a loved one at home, or their philosophy of touching the human spirit in each of their residents, the Silverado staff has been lovingly taught that love is greater than fear and that mantra guides the daily care of folks living with memory impairments from progressive neurological diseases such as Alzheimer's.

When a senior living campus has the ongoing involvement of

children -- from newborns to teens -- and the inclusion of many pets documented by a policy for the ratio of animals to residents, when daily routines are developed by the residents themselves, and when elders living with memory-impairment are active in the outside community, it has to be a Silverado campus. No one else does it this way, guided by love.

Silverado is a noisy place. People aren't here to rest or be silent, to slip quietly from the society that all too often doesn't want to hear their sounds. They come here to live.

And live life to the fullest regardless of diagnosis. "The Silverado Story" clearly underscores the disregard of diagnosis and the applause of humanness. The book is full of warm and witty stories of Loren and Steve as young men when Silverado was but a dream and the reader is equally engaged in the scores of eloquent tales from family members, residents and staff members who have come through the doors for more than a decade. Each moment of everyday life is enriched through spontaneous interactions and scheduled activities.

No one seems to be concerned with how well a resident once functioned; they are only concerned with the strengths he has today and the memories that are being recorded in the here and now.

"The Silverado Story" is not just for healthcare professionals but should be on bookshelves of any home where the occupants plan to grow old! It is a tome of splendid realities and heart-warming truths. We all can benefit from this very special story.

Joanne Koenig Coste
Author, "Learning to Speak Alzheimer's"

Preface

Central to the Silverado philosophy is the concept of love. Movingly elaborated in a deeply personal way, Loren Shook's epiphany after having established himself as a successful businessman has guided the practices at his Silverado Senior Living residences.

But also central to the success of Silverado Senior Living are two other concepts, acceptance and purpose. Acceptance of what the memory-impaired are not capable of allows one to accept and value what they CAN do. It also encourages treatment options other than psychoactive medications, which all too often dull the mind and spirit, producing listless, even vegetative states. Reliance on drugs also overlooks the likelihood that, in many instances, rebellion against being treated as less than human is the cause of their occasional aggression rather than behavior that needs to be "brought under control" by drugs.

In addition to acceptance -- and with it, respect -- is purpose. To paraphrase Nietzche, one who has a why can cope with any what. Sometimes the purpose can be caring for a pet; sometimes it can be forming a group like the Silverado Service Club, put together by some residents themselves for organizing volunteer activities to the community, like knitting blankets for newborns and delivering them (with staff assistance, of course) to a nearby hospital. Existential philosophy and psychology are built around the importance of people's need to construct meaning in their lives. Shook and Winner compellingly argue that memory-impaired people are not only capable of a search for meaning but that they need it as much as those of us whose cognitive abilities are not compromised by disease and inactivity – perhaps even more so.

Gerald C. Davison, Ph.D.
William & Sylvia Kugel Dean's Chair
Professor of Gerontology and Psychology
Dean, Leonard Davis School of Gerontology
Executive Director, Ethel Percy Andrus Gerontology Center,
University of Southern California

Introduction

Our vision in the mid-1990s was to create Silverado Senior Living as an organization that would change how the world cares for people with Alzheimer's and other memory-impairing diseases. It would be a place where residents would participate in a community with purpose and passion. The vision was "to give life" to the residents, their families and our associates serving them. In so doing, Silverado would transform the way society provides care to memory-impaired individuals and how others view them.

It was a bold vision for a company that opened its doors in just one location, with practices that drew skeptical looks from many of the experts at the time. And it turned out we were on the mark. Through the belief and commitment of staff, families and most of all, the residents, Silverado has blossomed. Every day, the people in our care inspire us and prove a splendid truth: When love guides us and we refuse to succumb to fear, extraordinary things can happen.

Everything in this book is true, although some names have been altered to protect privacy. *The Silverado Story* is the tale of many people over a long period of time who constantly believe they can change the world for the better.

Loren Shook & Stephen Winner

Chapter One
Prologue

May I have the courage today
To live the life that I would love
To postpone my dream no longer
But do at last what I came here for
And waste my heart on fear no more.

John O'Donoghue

At one of the lowest points of his life, Loren Shook went to a retreat high in the California mountains. When he came down two days later, he was not a changed man. He was a man who promised himself he would try to change.

Loren's stature at the time as a successful entrepreneur and chief executive made him the envy of many. He had fought to establish a place where people with Alzheimer's and other diseases that impair memory could live with meaning and his dream for Silverado Senior Living was now a flourishing reality.

But what most people didn't see was the sense of failure scorching his soul. His marriage was ending. Even now, years later, he has trouble finding the words to describe his feelings then, only saying he might have remained in that abyss if not for the support of his long-time friend and executive coach Vance Caesar, along with family and friends. As he did each year, Vance renewed his invitation to Loren to take part in a weekend men's retreat in the San Jacinto Mountains. Loren surprised himself by accepting after so often declining the offer.

On that Saturday, he and a dozen other business leaders arrived at a lodge perched between two expanses of towering rock. Loren couldn't help but notice the setting seemed to be nature's way of encouraging introspection. When Vance beckoned the men into a circle in the living room and began talking in a quiet tone about happiness, Loren was ready to listen.

Throughout the centuries, Vance began, great thinkers, philosophers, religious leaders -- from the renowned to those familiar only to scholars -- have said the two emotions at the human core are love and fear. All other feelings spring from them. "Those who have achieved the most happiness in their lives have generally done so because they based their decisions and actions on love rather than fear. They have acted in the best interests of the people around them instead of behaving from anger and defensiveness, which arise when we feel threatened or unsure."

Vance looked intently at each man. "Most of us grew up with fear, even if our parents didn't consciously intend it that way. It wasn't the A on your report card that got their attention; it was the C and what you had or hadn't done to get that grade. That was their own fear speaking, of course, and the insecurity bred by fear. If you were to fail, it meant they had failed, or so they thought."

As adults, we perpetuate our childhood experiences, Vance said. He was certain the men in the room had felt that fear and that it had shaped the countless decisions and actions leading to where they were now. They were all what society calls overachievers. But might they have accomplished more in the past and could they achieve more in the future by accepting love as their navigator?

Vance paused and then spoke of the issue that is hard for many men to voice, but that he knew dominated their thoughts.

"You will be happier in your personal life and you will find people are drawn to you if you choose to live your life based on love. You will develop better relationships. This is the decision you must make -- whether to change and let love be your guide or continue to live a life shaped by fear."

The words were like a lightning strike for Loren, revealing a truth about himself that he hadn't glimpsed before. The will to succeed, and to succeed by doing the right thing, had characterized his life from the earliest days of his impoverished and improbable childhood. No one could argue with that intention or its effectiveness. It had taken Loren, his family, the company he worked for and the one he founded very far.

But at this moment in the lodge, Loren realized there is only one way to truly know what the right thing to do is. It is by making choices and acting on the greatest positive emotion: Love.

As Loren reflected on what Vance had said, he wasn't sure he could commit to coping with his failing marriage in this manner, or that he would treat every future decision that way. But he felt if he were going to live by the philosophy – something he instantly knew he wanted to do – it would not be halfway. It would have to guide all aspects of his life, professional as well as personal. A phrase flashed in his mind. It would become his polestar.

Love is greater than fear.

On the drive down the mountain, Loren resolved to tell Silverado's executive team about the concept the following Monday during the customary monthly meeting. But when the company's vice presidents gathered in the corporate conference room, the normally punctual Loren twice retreated to his desk before summoning the courage to leave his office.

"They're going to think I'm nuts," he thought. "Guys don't talk about love. Loren, you're a chicken, a gutless wonder. You are letting yourself come from fear. You need to come from love. So you're going to bring it up."

And he did.

Surprised silence and impassive expressions greeted Loren's talk about *Love is greater than fear*. Later, Loren would recall a few faces turned ashen and others smiled cautiously when he finished by proposing that Silverado adopt the concept as its core operating principle. With Loren's prodding, discussion ensued and eventually, the executives reached a consensus: The idea was good, but it would be better if love weren't involved. Perhaps "like" or "strongly like" might take its place.

"But this is exactly the point," Loren said. "We're all afraid of the word love. Think about it: we want the staff to do the right thing with our residents and each other. That's such a silly phrase, really. 'Do the right thing.' How can they decide what's right in any given situation if we don't provide the criteria for determining it? But if we say you should serve residents and other staff from the standpoint of love, then it will be clear."

As the company grows, Loren continued, it will become harder for employees to understand and carry out the founding vision. That is true for any organization when it expands. "But if everyone at Silverado knows they are to act from love, they will naturally fulfill the vision every day."

Steve Winner, Silverado's co-founder, Chief of Culture and Senior Vice President, was intrigued by the concept and the teachings behind it. After the meeting, he went to the library to find out more and came home with an armload of books. "I enjoyed learning about it and I could quickly see how beneficial it would be for the company," Steve remembers.

Loren set about introducing *Love is greater than fear* throughout Silverado. He brought the same fire to this endeavor as he had to building the company from scratch. He dedicated much time to group training sessions and one-on-one conversations with staff. Some in management found the philosophy difficult to come to grips with "because of what it might lead to, the fear that comes of feeling you are giving up control to take a new approach," Loren recalls. "They would ask, 'Why risk this change when everything is going so well?'"

However, the certified nursing assistants, housekeepers, culinary staff, maintenance people and others who work most directly with residents responded without hesitation. Of course, we love them, they would say upon being told of the philosophy. That's why we're here.

Employees began saying that learning about *Love is greater than fear* was changing their lives at home as well as in the workplace. It helped them communicate with spouses and children, mend relationships damaged by anger and regret. Loren knew this principle had the power to improve the quality of life for everyone, regardless of how much money they made or what circumstances they experienced in their own lives. However even years later, he remains awed by its powerful reach.

He is convinced that *Love is greater than fear* can yield remarkable transformations on a wide scale. Professional associations, boards of directors, and individual executives at other companies frequently invite him to speak on the topic. He has heard from many that "I would love to do this at my business, but I would never dare" and this saddens him.

People who have known Loren a long time believe that *Love is greater than fear* has wrought a major change in him, more than he realizes. Loren's finely-tuned moral compass has never been in doubt. But he measures his words more carefully now and many times he softens his tone. He is quicker to trust and to forgive. Some have noticed that his body seems looser, in greater sync with his emotional and physical surroundings. It's as though he has shimmied out of a protective shell and is more open to the world.

Loren, single again, was on his first date with Suzanne, the woman he would later marry and with whom he would find a kind of happiness he had not known before.

During the salad course and main plate, he listened closely as Suzanne talked of her work as a nurse and how she had decided on her career as a young girl. Then Loren told her about Silverado, its vision of creating life for the memory impaired and why it mattered so much.

But, he said, you can't really understand Silverado without knowing what's at its center. When the waiter cleared away the entrees, Loren slid his chair beside Suzanne's. He found a scrap of paper in his billfold, smoothed it on the table and drew a diagram.

"Fear is on the left side of this spectrum and love is on the right," he told her. "Think of it as a scale, with fear at zero and love at 100. If you can make love-based choices 85 to 90 percent of the time, you have succeeded. It means that for you, love is greater than fear. This is what we believe, what we live by, at Silverado. It is what I have committed to work toward in my life."

Chapter Two
The Need to be Understood

*Whether we name divine presence synchronic-
ity, serendipity, or graced moment matters little.
What matters is the reality that our hearts have
been understood. Nothing is as real as a healthy
dose of magic which restores our spirits.*

Ralph Waldo Emerson

The glossy palomino accompanied Loren across the leafy grounds, horse and teenager matching their pace. As the pair neared the hospital, Loren saw an orderly roll Janet out through the entrance and onto the wide driveway. A doctor and two nurses gathered behind the wheelchair. It wasn't the first time Loren had noticed this patient. She was in her late twenties at the most, and she might have been pretty if her features displayed animation. Her head tilted slightly downward and although her eyes were open, her face was an alabaster mask of stillness. Her body was as motionless and rigid.

When Janet had been brought to Fairfax Hospital the previous week, she hadn't made a sound or flinched when a nurse inserted the needle into her wrist to give her fluids. A doctor came into her room, stood by her bed, and asked her questions that evoked no reaction. He took her right wrist and raised her arm above her head. When he let go, it stayed in this surely uncomfortable position, as if she were a department-store mannequin. After a few moments, the doctor gently clasped her arm again and slowly lowered it. Janet's was a classic case of catatonia, the unresponsive state a German physician first described in 1874.

Psychiatry blossomed as a profession in the twentieth century, but on this day in the early 1970s, scientists had not yet developed the drugs that would become standard treatment for mental disorders. Fairfax Hospital was a sanitarium where the staff treated catatonia, depression, schizophrenia, dementia, and other maladies of the mind by examining their patients' life stories. They sought clues to tell them who these people were before illness gripped their psyches, what had motivated them, what had mattered to them. Then they used the information to design treatments that were unique to each person.

For example, a Fairfax social worker questioned Janet's family closely when she arrived and learned she had always loved

CATATONIA

Catatonia is not necessarily a diagnosis but rather a descriptive term for a presentation of a variety of symptoms.
See silveradostory.com/catatonia

horses. As a child, Janet lived down the road from a farm. Each day after school, she went there to curry the stallion and two mares, muck out their stalls, and refresh their water. In exchange, she was allowed to ride them. Growing into adulthood and moving far from the farm ended this beloved ritual.

Loren was not surprised when a nurse told him to go to the pasture and bring a horse back for Janet. Fairfax Hospital's approach to psychiatric treatment was a way of life for him. At 19, Loren had been working at Fairfax for four years. He was a "gofer," mopping floors, helping patients with showers, washing dishes, raking leaves, and relieving nursing staff during their breaks. Whatever needed to be done at a given moment, Loren was expected to do. His aunt and uncle owned the 20-acre facility. Loren and his brother and parents had moved into a two-room house on the hospital grounds after their chicken farm failed.

The hospital kept the palomino, named Heidi, and two other horses among a menagerie that included dogs, peacocks, pheasants, and chickens. Fragrant gardens, meandering paths, expansive rolling lawns shaded under a canopy of maple and oak trees, and a stream so clear that thousands of salmon spawned annually decorated the sprawling grounds. The verdant setting was another treatment tool at Fairfax Hospital. Fresh air, nature's rhythms and the company of animals reconnected patients to the world in an invigorating way.

Each time Loren approached the pasture, Heidi would come to the fence to nuzzle him. The palomino was what you would call a "people horse," stepping forward for caresses and carrots while her pasture-mates retreated. That's why Loren had chosen to slip the halter over her head on this day. If a horse needed to be brought to meet a woman with catatonia, he believed one with an interest in humans would be best.

With Loren still at her side, Heidi clopped onto the pavement and halted in front of Janet. The sun was bright, but Janet didn't blink, even as the big horse drew close and stopped.

There was silence, a long hush in which even the birds seemed to hold their breath.

Suddenly, Janet stretched out her arm, the same arm the doctor raised and lowered. She touched Heidi with a finger. Then, she laid her whole hand on the palomino's warm side and began stroking her. After a few moments, she used both arms to push herself up and out of the wheelchair. She grasped Heidi's face, and leaned in close to speak to her.

Her tone was soft, yet urgent. Loren and the others couldn't make out what she was saying. They didn't try. This was a private communication of the souls, between a long-mute woman and the empathic horse that brought her back to the world.

Three weeks later, Janet walked out of Fairfax Hospital and went home, her spirit and life restored. Loren never saw her again. But the conversation he couldn't quite hear on the driveway that day would echo decades later.

A dog jumps a quick barking dance for a biscuit dangling just a whisker outside his reach.

Rubber soles squeak as a grinning toddler makes a dash across shiny tiles.

Chairs scrape up to a table and hammers begin pounding nails into wood in an unsyncopated tap, tap-tap, tap.

A male voice calls out: "We need you at men's club", and another answers: "I'm coming, I'm coming." Out of sight, drums thump in varying tones and rhythms. The front door swing open with a whoosh. Three teenagers spill in, all talking at once.

Silverado Senior Living is a noisy place.

People aren't here to rest or to be silent, to slip quietly from the society that all too often doesn't want to hear their sounds.

They come here to *live*.

They are people with Alzheimer's disease, vascular dementia, Parkinson's, and a host of other memory-impairing illnesses with names that confer a sense of the alien on fathers, mothers, husbands, wives, sisters, brothers, and close friends. As their condition progresses, garbling their speech and reason, they become strangers to those around them and to themselves.

Your loving spouse of 50 years, the parent you relied on, the sibling whose tandem experience with your own makes the world familiar: these people are gone.

Or so it seems until you step into Silverado.

Because at its core, there's the belief – no, call it knowledge based on experience – that if embraced by the wider world, Silverado will transform the lives of all those who have memory-impairment and enrich the souls of everyone else. It's an insight that puts aside fear and replaces it with love.

What Silverado knows is that the human spirit glows until we take our last breath. While memory-impairment erodes the spirit's ability to express itself through words and actions considered normal, it doesn't mean the spirit is not present. It still shines, but speaks differently. And if outsiders can't understand this different kind of communication, then we must work together to figure it out. It's like learning a new language. Once you begin grasping what seemed incomprehensible, new vistas, new possibilities open.

A memory-impairing disease is tragic, yes. You absorb the weight of its despair if it touches you through a loved parent, spouse, partner, sibling, friend. But in devoting time, effort, and love to detecting this new way to communicate, to accepting the memory-impaired as they are and to building new lives and relationships for and with them, we advance our own humanity, our own purpose. This is the vision of Silverado.

What makes life worth living? We are each a patchwork quilt of individual likes, dislikes, ambitions, desires, experiences, and genetic potpourri. But when you lay the quilts side by side and examine them, you see the stitching that unites the squares.

In all of us, there is the need to love and be loved. A need to be understood and appreciated, to surge through the day with purpose, bask in the warmth and light of sunshine, connect with animals, children, flowers, and simple pleasures the earth yields up to us. These are the things that feed our spirit.

Silverado knows these needs never change, regardless how altered a person appears to be by Alzheimer's disease or any other memory disorder.

For those of us with unimpaired memory, life is linear. We're born; we grow into children, teenagers, adults. Last year, this year, yesterday, today, tomorrow, this happened and that happened. But for people with Alzheimer's and similar conditions, today could be 20 years ago. An adult child is mistaken for a long-deceased mother. When those we love start stepping off the straight line, we try desperately to refocus them to

WHAT IS ALZHEIMER'S

Alzheimer's disease (pronounced Alz-hi-merz) is a progressive, degenerative disease that attacks the brain and results in impaired memory, thinking and behavior. See silveradostory.com/ alzheimers

normal. No, today is Tuesday. I'm not your mother; I'm your daughter. Don't you remember you already ate lunch?

When we realize we can't fix their memories, many of us turn away, withdrawing into our own pain. What's the point of trying to connect when they won't remember, anyway? What's the point of anything, other than keeping these frail and confused people safe, comfortable, clean, and fed?

Silverado is a memory-care organization that knows the vision isn't really about memory. It's about reaching and nurturing the human spirit inside each memory-impaired person. It doesn't matter what the day of the week is. What matters is that the day gives meaning.

How does Silverado do this?

Animals and children: They're central to what Silverado calls the living environment that links all humans to the world. The glorious thing to understand is that the memory-impaired don't need linear thoughts and words to connect with this joy. Touch, hugs, smiles, and laughter are the language here.

At least one dog and one cat for every 25 residents. One bird, or more, for every four people who reside at a Silverado community. A burbling tank with colorful fish for every 40.

Who would expect that required minimum numbers of resident animals would be a fundamental rule in memory care? But Silverado's 40-page copyrighted pet-care manual spells the regulations out clearly. That barking dog leaping for a treat is one of more than 400 non-humans, from canines and cats to rabbits, guinea pigs, miniature horses, and even a kangaroo, living permanently in Silverado's communities. They're joined by pets that move in with residents and by others who accompany staff to work each day.

The child barreling through a living room and the teens arriving in a chatty swarm embody another tenet. The company encourages employees to bring their children to work with them. So you see infants slumbering in residents' laps and toddlers taking their first steps in Silverado's hallways. School buses chug up in front of Silverado's communities and drop off youngsters who burst inside to spend the afternoon participating in activities alongside residents, helping care for the pets, or sitting quietly to study.

Purpose feeds the spirit, as well. A man who has always loved woodworking hasn't lost his passion for meaningful activity. What he no longer possesses is the ability to express his interest in ways we recognize. At Silverado, he won't craft his wood projects alone. Other residents and staff will work next to him, because a passion shared with friends satisfies even more. This understanding under-lies the "club concept," in which activity groups form to reflect the interests of those currently living at Silverado. There's the drum-ming circle, for instance, where residents come together to thump out rhythms in an expression of primacy that humans have engaged in for ages.

THE CLUB CONCEPT

For those with memory-impair-ment the idea of participating in a "club" is more familiar than a group. This concept promotes membership, holding a special position, and some exclusivity which supports self-esteem. See silveradostory.com/club

These activities reflect the interests of adults. Residents build woodworks. They garden, cook, create music, paint. They consider current events. They do not toss balloons, swaddle dolls, or gaze at cartoons on television – unless they've always enjoyed cartoons.

To the non-memory-impaired, the changes wrought by memory disorder seem to turn grown-ups into children, and so they're given childish games and toys. This practice dulls the spirit. It's also the first step toward quarantining the memory-impaired in a social space that is not normal. They start to appear as a less-than-human group whose rights to soul-affirming care, even to the common courtesy of being looked in the eye and addressed rather than ignored, quickly erode.

The relief, the pleasure, the dignity of normal: this is part of *life* at Silverado.

More than five million Americans currently live with Alzheimer's or another memory-impairing disease, according to the Alzheimer's Association. Nearly 10 million of their family members and friends are caring for them at home, a loving duty that can last several years, a decade, or even longer. Doctors diagnose a new case of Alzheimer's every 70 seconds. With the population's increasing aging, as many as 16 million Americans could develop memory impairment within four decades. The worldwide figure may exceed 115 million.

Public policy and health experts call the rise in memory-impairing diseases an epidemic. They hope this word will galvanize America's attention and action. It's a well-intentioned effort to convey the issue's magnitude. But of course, unlike the plague, influenza, polio, and other illnesses that have terrorized humanity for centuries, memory-impairment is not contagious.

FRONTOTEMPORAL DEMENTIA

The frontotemporal dementias (FTD) are a group of degenerative brain disorders that share many clinical features. See silveradostory.com/ftd

As a society, though, we treat people with Alzheimer's and other memory disorders as if they have something the rest of us might catch. When they become less able to participate in normal life and their behavior strays from the linear path, we isolate them behind drawn shades and closed doors at home or within institutions where few but staff and dutiful family ever appear.

As with contagious diseases, we do this primarily to protect ourselves. We don't worry we'll catch their condition, but their memory-impairment frightens us, confuses us, makes us angry. Sometimes, what they do and say repulses us.

But when we stop nurturing their human spirit through meaningful connection with the world, we hasten their decline. Depression, loneliness, feelings of worthlessness aggravate their symptoms and their overall health. We're cutting off the oxygen that feeds the inner flame. Their spirits rebel, flicker, and die.

America's propensity to solve all ills with a pill contributes to the sad lives that so many memory-impaired endure. It's easiest and seems natural in today's world to load more prescriptions into their bodies in an effort to "get their behavior under control." So they swallow as many as 15 different drugs a day, stupefying the spirit. Those who don't sink into an almost constant sleep often lash out verbally and physically. What's mistaken for incurable aggression in the memory-impaired is the spirit's cry of protest against the regimen that suffocates their self-expression.

Research primarily seeks to find a pharmacological cure for memory-impairment and a way to prevent it. This quest dominates media coverage of Alzheimer's and shapes the public discussion. Silverado strongly supports this research. But the organization is also passionately leading the way on improving the daily lives of those with memory impairment in the here and now.

What if as a society we overcame our fears of Alzheimer's disease and responded to it with love? What if this disease represents an opportunity? What if we accepted and embraced those with memory impairments? We would find out what Silverado experiences every day: Our own spirit flourishes and we evolve through selfless love and service to the memory-impaired.

Tom arrived in a wheelchair, head and body leaning to one side, his skin like yellowing tissue paper loosely draped over bones. As

Sheila rolled him through wide bright hallways, she spoke gently in welcome, explaining where he was going and what he could expect. But only his wife Dorothy, walking alongside him, responded. Tom had not said anything in a long time. Nor had he eaten or flickered any notice of the world through eyes that seemed permanently shut.

Tom had been in a hospital for the past few weeks. Physicians couldn't pinpoint the cause of his nearly vegetative state. He was in his eighties and his Alzheimer's disease was tangled with a skein of other medical issues. The doctors told Dorothy that Tom had just a few days left to live, maybe a week or two. He should leave the hospital for a place to spend his last days. On this morning, an ambulance delivered Tom to the Silverado Senior Living community where Sheila worked.

A large window brought sunshine and a vista of the community's blooming backyard into the room chosen for him. Sheila didn't know if Tom would ever open his eyes again, but she positioned his bed so he had a view of the outdoors. Once Sheila tucked Tom in, she and Dorothy turned toward the dresser to unpack his suitcase.

The two women talked quietly, with Dorothy occasionally falling silent as she folded the clothing that was as much a part of her life as her husband's. There was the red flannel shirt – practically Tom's uniform on weekend mornings – and the beige cardigan he wore while reading on their patio.

Suddenly, the sheets rustled. The bed shifted with a small thud.

"Was that a horse I just saw?"

Sheila and Dorothy turned. Tom was sitting up, stretching forward toward the window, eyes wide in a blue gleam. Sheila went to the window to open it and lean out. Two small horses, one silvery and the other black with grey flecks, were sauntering along further down in the yard. She realized the pair had just walked right past the room. Sheila looked back at Tom. Dorothy was clasping Tom's hand to her cheek and she stooped down to his face.

"I never thought I would hear your voice again," she told him.

Then she gazed up at Sheila.

"My husband has always loved horses," she said.

Tom spent much of the following afternoon in Silverado's garden. There, he relished Dorothy's company and velvety nuzzles by Hocus Pocus and Lil' Rascal, the miniature horses who passed by Tom's window on the way to their stalls in Silverado's backyard. The man who doctors predicted would soon pass noiselessly from the world confounded their expectations. Tom's memory remained impaired and his body fragile, but his spirit glowed again. When Sheila recalls how she would see Tom and his wife sitting together in the sunlight, chatting and laughing, she smiles. She remains inspired by what she witnessed.

"Tom's family had tried everything before he came here," Sheila said. "His wife Dorothy felt that she had lost Tom well before he passed away. She didn't realize that while Tom's eyes looked like they were closed, he had them open just enough that his spirit could still watch the world."

Dorothy never thought a pair of horses could accomplish what the doctors hadn't been able to do for her husband. Then she and Tom came to Silverado.

Some people discover their mission early in life. Others accumulate experiences over decades. In their middle years, or after, they realize these events are threads of many colors waving a tapestry of purpose.

At the age of 19, Loren Shook was working at his aunt and uncle's psychiatric hospital when he witnessed a horse awakening a woman from catatonia. Few people would forget such a sight and Loren never did. More than 35 years afterwards, his voice quickened as he described the moment during a conversation in his office at the company he founded, Silverado Senior Living.

"I knew what I was seeing was important," he said. "But as a teenager, I couldn't have told you what my life's purpose was."

It was only later, as an adult with a successful career already behind him, that Loren came to understand he has always wanted to give life the way he and Heidi did that day, to restore it, to people whose spirits are being smothered.

Chapter Three
Connecting with the Human Spirit

We do not believe in ourselves until someone reveals that deep inside us something is valuable, worth listening to, worthy of our trust, sacred to our touch. Once we believe in ourselves we can risk curiosity, wonder, spontaneous delight or any experience that reveals the human spirit.

Ralph Waldo Emerson

Jean slid under the hedge, cramming as far under its spiky branches as she could. Lying on her back, she grabbed fistfuls of leaves and piled them over her legs, which didn't quite fit beneath the bush. Then she dropped a last handful over her face. Jean didn't want to be seen and she didn't want to see others.

The moist leaves molded to her cheeks, her chin, and her eyelids. Their sweet and earthy aroma could have been soothing, but Jean was not a woman to be quickly calmed. She did a good job camouflaging herself in Silverado's back garden and it wasn't easy for Maryam to find her.

"Jean, why did you disappear on us?" asked Maryam, kneeling down and gently brushing the leaves away.

"The police dogs were chasing me," Jean said. "Those men with the black masks were with them and telling them to catch me."

She paused and then said, "How dare they? How dare they come after me like this?"

Just after breakfast that morning, Jean had noticed several other Silverado residents walking with two of the community's dogs. It sparked a hallucination and Jean fled out the nearest door, frantic to find a place to hide from her imagined pursuers.

Jean had memory impairment. For several years, her family doctor had waved off Jean's increasing lapses of recollection as "just old age." Until, three weeks prior, her condition was revealed in a startlingly public way.

The day before attending a political convention, Jean made it known she planned to make her entrance in a white winter suit, dressy white hat, and designer jewelry, in keeping with her customarily regal style. But rather than arrive with studied panache, she burst into the meeting hall dressed in sweatpants and slippers, cradling a stuffed green frog wearing a Santa hat. She dashed over to a group of acquaintances and pleaded for their help. She was having car trouble, she said in a frantic tone. When they went outside, they found her vehicle in the middle of the parking lot. Its engine was running, all four doors were open and jewelry was strewn across the back seat.

Convention organizers summoned an ambulance. In the emergency room, physicians diagnosed frontal lobe dementia. Less prevalent than Alzheimer's disease, the condition is often associated with hallucinations, as are anger and aggression. When Jean left the hospital, she moved into Silverado.

Several days after she arrived, Jean grabbed a cane and smashed the Christmas tree in the lobby. She hurled a cup of hot coffee – saucer included – at a caregiver who stopped to chat with her. Were Jean living in almost any place other than Silverado, she would have been quickly administered a slew of tranquilizing medications.

But at Silverado, her outbursts were not seen as the senseless symptoms of a memory-impairing disease. Yes, the condition was a part of Jean, but it was just one part. Jean was also a person of opinion, ambition, longing, and more that had collected within her for more than eight decades of life. Silverado wasn't going to "treat Jean's dementia," something that by most definitions would have focused on drugging her into docility. Silverado was going to reach Jean's spirit.

"We don't silence our residents," said Loren Shook of the people in his organization's care. "We don't smother their voices, smother their spirits. We listen to them. If we listen to them closely, if we watch and observe what their bodies express through gestures, we can understand how to connect with their human spirit. That enables us to provide the care that's best for them."

Who was Jean when she came to Silverado? She was a businesswoman, an owner of commercial buildings, the holder of a real estate license. Starting in her teen years and throughout her life, Jean participated in a dizzying array of community groups and she invariably ascended to their presidencies: Soroptimist, business & professional women, historical society, town bicentennial committee, to name only a few of her activities.

As a child, she licked stamps and stuffed envelopes for presidential candidate Wendell Wilkie. Her passion for Republican politics was so fervent that she twice served as a delegate to the GOP presidential nominating convention. She followed political news incessantly, keeping her television tuned to talk shows 24 hours a day.

Jean collected shoes – she owned 100 pairs – and had acquired 600 hats. She married five times. She was never an easy person, those closest to her are quick to say. They describe her as authoritative, in charge, always in control, always *taking* control.

A few days after Jean's dash into Silverado's garden, Maryam, who is the resident engagement director at Jean's community, stopped by her room. She noticed the shade on the lamp by Jean's bed bore jagged dark pink stripes with the hue and consistency of lipstick.

"Jean, did you do this?" Maryam asked.

Jean nodded and said: "Look in the closet. I've written inside there."

Maryam opened it. The same pink hue scrawled words of anger inside the door and along the walls.

"I could see that Jean's spirit was expressing itself," Maryam said a year later. "Jean had always been so independent, so strong. She was angry because she felt she had lost her authority and control. Her memory-impairment had taken away the life that had meant everything to her. To provide the care that would be best for Jean, we would need to give that authority and control back to her."

A way to do that, Maryam believed, was by involving Jean in Silverado's activities – not simply in the activities themselves, but in operating the entire program.

"We started by asking her opinion," Maryam said. "We asked her to observe the classes and clubs we have for residents and to tell us what she thought of them. We asked her to tell us if she thought there were ways they could be improved."

Little by little, Jean became intrigued. "I told her, 'I need your help. We need someone strong like you to help us with the program,'" Maryam said. Jean began to assist with some events. Maryam assigned her a desk in the activities department and provided her with a name badge identical to those worn by the community's staff.

These days, Jean sits in on interviews of potential employees for the activities department. She creates binders of photos and information on suggested activities and she runs the community's flower-arranging club.

"Not every class is smooth," Maryam said, "but many of them are."

As Jean's involvement with the activities program increased, her outbursts disappeared. Despite her memory-impairment, a year after coming to Silverado, Jean is able to reflect on her transition. She fled into Silverado's garden that day because she felt that "I was being held against my will and I tried to hide under the leaves to hide away. That was my way to run away and rebel. I have always been a very independent person."

Being part of the activities program has made all the difference. "Running classes gives me a sense of fulfillment. I can do something and be appreciated by others. I had authority all my life in different clubs and organizations, giving me authority here gave me that back."

Working with flowers is important to Jean because "looking at a beautiful arrangement, you can't help but feel satisfied that you created it."

Jean no longer collects hats or shoes, she doesn't want more things. She never watches the television her daughters installed in her room and recently asked that it be taken out. She doesn't have time for it.

Her transformation has surprised and gratified her daughters Teri and Linda.

"She has so much pleasure with the flower arranging and the classes," Teri said. "She must be remembering and revisiting a part of her identity that meant a lot early in her life, before she became wrapped up in so many activities and politics."

Linda added: "For our mother, memory impairment hasn't meant the end of her life. It has meant a new stage of her life, one that has been tremendously satisfying."

Words are just one way to connect with a person's spirit at Silverado, where touching the flame within each resident has always been at the core of its care. With Jean, caregivers listened to what she had to say and were able to draw her out through questions. They interpreted her life story. They offered her new possibilities and saw how she expressed herself through her choices. The process of reaching the spirit of anyone is not a one-size-fits-all practice and is even more difficult with the memory-impaired. It takes time, it can discourage and frustrate.

For Henry, the connection happened one morning when he noticed work outside his window. He came to Silverado saying little. He wouldn't leave the chair by his bed. He shifted his gaze down each time he was invited to join in an activity. When staff brought him breakfast on a tray, he turned away. Later in the morning, they would find it almost untouched.

One day, several Silverado residents and staff moved a small barn into the community's courtyard and began painting it. They were preparing for an event with a Western theme. After so many days of apathy, Henry was suddenly interested. He came outside, pulled up a chair, sat down, crossed one leg over another and watched the activity for several hours, his face alert with a slightly appraising expression.

Why did Henry's spirit come to life? Silverado staff knew Henry had run his own company for many years. This man who rejected every overture might respond to the bustle of a work site. So, when the barn needed to be painted, they made sure Henry would see the activity.

"For the next few days, we asked Henry if he would take his breakfast in the courtyard and keep an eye on what was going on," explained Carole, administrator of the community where Henry resides. "We could see that this was a person who had always supervised work and that this mattered to him. The change in Henry from that day on was enormous."

Understanding how to connect with the spirit of the memory-impaired wasn't obvious at the outset for David. He is a chaplain with Silverado Hospice. His first meeting with those in his charge often comes when they can no longer open their eyes or speak.

"I thought to myself, 'It's one thing to provide nursing care to a memory-impaired person at the end of life, but what does it mean to be a chaplain when a person no longer appears to be there?'"

Through his training and his experience at Silverado, David said he knows now that "people in a remote state, whether it's a coma or deep dementia, are still people and we can reach them."

Often, David starts by matching his breathing to the patient's pace. After establishing a bond through this shared cadence, he adds words.

THE HISTORY OF HOSPICE

The word "hospice" comes from the Latin word hospes meaning to host a guest or stranger. See silveradostory.com/hospice

"I can feel the rhythm of your breath. I can see that your eyes are moving under your eyelids. If it's all right with you, I would like to hold your hand for a while."

Time and again, David has seen how presence, focus, and touch spark the spiritual connection, which expresses itself through small, but intensely compelling, signs. One example among many was his contact with a man in the last stages of Parkinson's.

"As I held his hand, it had strong tremors from his disease. I began to talk to him, about the transition from this life to the next stage. After a while, despite the tremors, I could feel that he was squeezing my hand. It was an important and powerful moment."

"Touching the spirit of the memory-impaired at life's end has enriched me tremendously and given me a better understanding of myself," David says. Silverado associates throughout the company say that the spiritual connection with those in their care changes their own lives for the better.

The distressing symptoms of memory impairment and its inevitable downward progression are like a thief who slips into our lives and robs us of the person we were and the people we knew. How is it possible that diseases affecting memory can change us in a positive way?

"I think people don't understand how nourishing it is to our minds and to our emotions to connect with another human spirit," Carole said. "This connection is something we fundamentally need as human beings, but we're losing it in modern life. When I can focus on another person, when it's just the two of us communicating with each other, regardless of whether we use words, it feeds every piece of my soul and the soul of the other person."

She added that she is thankful every day that Silverado's residents allow her to have this connection with them. "They do so much more for me than I could ever do for them."

Carole's work with the memory-impaired has spanned two

decades. She holds what many would consider a renegade view: that this disease, while heartbreaking, can also be liberating. Released from the inhibitions of social conventions, many Silverado residents try their hand at activities they would never have considered before.

A man who rarely stepped into his kitchen at home joins the resident cooking club. A woman builds a birdhouse, even though she used to think of herself as all thumbs. Add to that the resident who was always told she was tone-deaf and now is part of the community chorus. Those around her encourage her to vocalize louder.

At Silverado, her spirit has the freedom to sing its song.

Chapter Four
The Power of Normal

Simply the thing that I am shall make me live.
William Shakespeare

People who walk into Silverado for the first time might be surprised to see a group of men in the living room drinking beer and watching a football game on television.

But they wouldn't think twice if they saw the same thing in someone's home.

Silverado's view is there's no reason to change what residents normally like to do just because they've moved into a memory-impairment community. In fact, *not* changing is central to Silverado's care.

This practice is called normalization. Bengt Nirje, the Swedish humanitarian and scholar who formulated the concept, defined the word with a poet's grace:

Normalization means ... A normal rhythm of the day.
You get out of bed in the morning ...

You get dressed,
And leave the house for school or work,
You don't stay home …
The day is not a monotonous 24 hours with every minute endless.
You eat at normal times of the day and in a normal fashion …
Not in bed, but at a table;
Not early in the afternoon for the convenience of the staff.
Normalization means…A normal rhythm of the week.
You live in one place,
Go to work in another,
And participate in leisure activities in yet another …
Normalization means…A normal rhythm of the year …
Seasonal changes bring with them a variety
Of types of food, work, cultural events, sports,
Leisure activities.
Just think… We thrive on seasonal changes.
Normalization means…Having a range of choices,
Wishes and desires respected and considered.

Born in 1924, Nirje joined the Swedish Red Cross as a young man. In 1956, the organization sent him to Austria to assist Hungarians who fled their country's revolution and crowded into military barracks there. Nirje also visited camps throughout Europe where World War II refugees had been living for more than a decade. What he saw marked him deeply:

"This period taught me that when you are a refugee, you have a past that is gone and does not count in your new country. No one cares about you … nobody trusts you. Your past is really gone, and you really know nothing about the future. Your situation is bleak, uncertain and anonymous. Such a situation can create a very unhealthy climate and dark moods … There is no place for you, your family, or your few belongings. You have to be strong, even if you are competent and not intellectually disabled. But you can become mentally 'wounded' and socially handicapped."

Red Cross next assigned Nirje to raise funds for children in Sweden who had cerebral palsy. The organization wanted to move the youngsters out of large impersonal institutions into settings that were more like home. Nirje was struck by how the children's lives paralleled those of the refugees.

"They could not be certain where they were going, their present position was bleak, and they had very little power. They enjoyed no independence … They were dependent, and their state of dependence humiliated them. From these experiences I got my first inkling of the meaning of independence and the right to self-determination."

From there, Nirje grew to believe in what he called normalization: that living with the same customs of society as a whole and with personal choice is everyone's right. When a group of people is treated as less than normal, whether because of their physical, mental, or economic conditions, their spirits wither.

In 1969, a United States presidential commission studying the living conditions of people with mental disabilities cited normalization in a landmark report. The document brought fresh attention to the large facilities where many mentally handicapped Americans had been sent. What emerged was shocking: media reports of people living nearly naked, soiled by their own waste, showered as a group by cold water from a hose, locked alone in barren rooms with only small barred windows for light.

A push began in the mental health industry to move developmentally-disabled people out of the horrific institutions and into small group homes in cities and towns where they could become part of society. At the same time, psychologist Dr. Wolf Wolfensberger extended Nirje's work on normalization to consider the issue of devalued people.

Wolfensberger was born in Germany in 1934. During World War II, he was sent to the countryside to stay out of the way of bombs falling on German cities. He later moved to the United States and

NORMALIZATION

The principle of normalization aims to refute the idea that people who have disabilities should be kept separate from society.
See silveradostory.com/normal

earned a Ph.D. in psychology, with a focus on developmental disability and special education. The author of over 40 books and monographs and more than 250 chapters and articles, Dr. Wolfensberger's career has earned worldwide renown. Throughout his working life, he has focused on a question clearly sparked by his experiences as a child in a war-torn nation. How can people who are seemingly good do bad things to others?

Dr. Wolfensberger determined that such violations occur when groups of people become devalued in their society. Once a person is regarded as not normal, he or she loses worth in the eyes of those considered normal. From there, it's all too easy to treat someone in ways that would be otherwise unthinkable.

This disregard can begin with an act of discourtesy. Left unchecked, it can slide downward with surprising speed to physical, verbal, and emotional abuse – even to deprivation of life itself. Like Nirje, Dr. Wolfensberger has continued to center his work with normalization on the developmentally disabled and the concept is now widely understood in that field.

Silverado Senior Living is the only memory-care organization founded on normalization and its use grew directly from the work of Nirje and Dr. Wolfensberger.

At Silverado you will never see a coloring book and crayons lying on a table in front of a silver-haired man.

You won't spot a lady walking down the hall at three in the afternoon clad in a bathrobe and slippers.

You will not come across laundered undergarments piled immodestly on the top of a dresser, rather than folded and put away where they belong. You won't see a hand-scrawled note taped to the wall by a bed that says, "He needs toileting frequently."

Consider the gentleman's age, the time of day the woman is strolling in the hallway, the personal dignity with which we all like to live: those things *are not normal*.

MEMORY BOXES

As you walk down the halls of Silverado Senior Living, "memory boxes" - lovely cabinets filled with memorabilia of many lives and many special people surround you.
See silveradostory.com/boxes

However, you *will* see at Silverado football fans gathered in front of a game with brews and chips, sharing a lifelong Sunday afternoon passion.

You'll notice ladies dressed in the daytime attire they've always worn. When they head out from their rooms to participate in programs and activities, they carry their purses with them, as any woman might upon leaving her house.

When you visit residents in their rooms, you'll find that intimate apparel is tucked out of sight and the walls are free of demeaning notes. In their place are family pictures, cherished artwork, souvenirs from special trips, and other meaningful items that he or she has brought to Silverado. They represent the arc of normal living.

A memory box just outside the room holds mementoes testifying to individual interests and achievements. Gold records shine in the display by the room of a music industry executive. A baseball mitt and trophies are the cherished possessions of a resident who made a name for himself in minor league ball and might have reached the big leagues if not for a bum elbow. They're there for everyone to see.

Disease of the brain may have brought on a host of changes, but it has not sent people back to childhood. At times, people seeking positions as caregivers at Silverado have worked with the memory-impaired elsewhere will say, "I treat the people I care for the way I would treat my own children." While they mean well, it reflects the attitude that's common not only in society as a whole, but also throughout the senior living profession that a person with memory impairment is childlike.

Silverado's adherence to normalization is so stringent that teams of employees conduct normalization audits, which means that staff from one Silverado community will visit another. They devote an entire day to touring, making sure no aspect of operations or resident care has strayed from normality.

"We do this from a constructive criticism standpoint," said a resident engagement director who recently participated in one of the inspections. "When you work in a community every day, it could be hard to notice if something isn't quite right. This is really bringing in a fresh set of eyes to make sure nothing has been overlooked."

For nearly two decades after her husband passed away, Maria lived by herself in an apartment. Her three grown children stopped in nearly every day, which enabled her to continue the routine that has been central to her adult life: cooking meals and chatting in Spanish. A native of Argentina, Maria has always been most comfortable with that language.

As Maria neared 80, her family noticed changes in her behavior, which were ultimately diagnosed as symptoms of memory-impairment. She moved into a senior living community where the staff tried to involve her in sing-alongs and games with other residents.

"It was a nice place and the people there worked hard to get her to participate, but she didn't want to," her son Al recalled. Maria cried often and became restless, unable to sit still for more than a few minutes.

After her condition declined to the point of hospitalization, Maria's family brought her to Silverado. From interviews with Maria and her family, Silverado's staff realized how central meal preparation has been to her life, as is speaking Spanish. This represented normal living for Maria. Participating in group activities and regularly conversing in English – no one at the previous senior community spoke Spanish – did not.

Maria had lost her normal.

Once Silverado's staff understood what was so critically missing from Maria's life, they restored it. The culinary staff, which includes several Spanish speakers, invited her to help out in the kitchen. Maria accepted the offer and began setting the tables for dinner.

During ensuing months, she happily took on more responsibilities. Now, she prepares the tables for all three daily meals. She chops ingredients and garnishes plates, chatting in Spanish with her kitchen colleagues all the while.

To those who work alongside Maria in the kitchen, she is a colleague and friend, a normal part of a team. To others in her

Silverado community, she's a smiling and active presence, busy with the regular routines of her day. The fact she has impaired memory is just another part of what makes her an individual, as does her ability to speak Spanish, her preference for cooking rather than sports, and a hundred other such personal traits, choices, and talents.

No one can remember the last time Maria cried.

"My mother is back to her old ways," her son Al said. "She has purpose. She has been given back the life that she knew and that mattered to her. It's almost like she has adopted a new family to care for."

That is the power of normal.

Chapter Five
A Different Point of View

*Whatever course you decide upon, there is always
someone to tell you that you are wrong. There
are always difficulties arising which tempt you to
believe that your critics are right. To map out a
course of action and follow it to an end requires
courage.*

Ralph Waldo Emerson

A small boy and a dog crossed a field under a black blanket of sky
scattered with pinpricks of starlight and a crescent slit of moon.
It was the kind of darkness only possible in a place many miles from
streetlamps and passing cars.

While Loren and his hound Duke barely had enough light to
see where they were going, they knew the way. He was only five,
but every day, Loren and the dog walked a distance of eight football
fields to feed 500 chickens. In a family that raised fowl for a living in
rural Washington State, Loren's duty was to come straight home after
kindergarten and head for the coops.

On this day, Loren didn't leave school immediately. The temp-
tation to join the other children on the playground after class was
just too great. When he did return home, it was dark. His mother
gave him a long look and said nothing. But while Loren was washing
his hands for dinner, his father came home from his job at the feed

mill and she told him the chickens hadn't been fed. When Loren came into the kitchen, his father said in a tone that was not unkind, but was firm: "Son, you have to go feed those chickens, right now."

Loren took his jacket off the hook by the door. He stepped outside and picked up the flashlight lying on a worktable under the eaves of the house. Duke appeared at his side. As Loren pulled the door shut, his father disappeared into the bedroom to change his coveralls. His mother turned back toward the soup bubbling on the stove.

Loren looked into the inky night and swallowed hard. He clicked the flashlight on, pointed its thin beam forward and began walking in the customary direction. The darkness turned hedges into gargoyles. Rustling squirrels became monsters' footsteps. Duke's pant was the only familiar sound in this alien landscape.

After what felt like the longest walk of Loren's life, he and Duke reached the coops and Loren made quick work of feeding the chickens. Then the pair set off on the frightening trek back to the farmhouse. When they arrived, Duke slipped off to the barn and Loren went into the kitchen. His father was sitting at the table, his mother ladling the soup into his bowl. "I got the chickens fed, Dad," Loren said. His father nodded an indication for Loren to wash his hands again and come to the table.

Loren and his father never talked about that night, not even when Loren grew into an adult who could measure the unusual fact of being sent alone on such a walk at the age of five. When you ask him about it, he tells you "I learned a lesson from this, about responsibility, what you owe your family. When you have duties, you can't shirk them."

He believes now, after years of reflection, that his dad must have followed him silently that night to ensure he was safe.

Loren's father always dreamed of owning his own chicken farm. When Loren was a year old, his family moved from Iowa to Washington on a quest to make this desire come true. They bought a farm that was a boy's paradise with its two dozen acres of pasture, hills, trees and sprawling house. His parents took jobs to supplement their farming income. But they considered the measure temporary, something to tide them over until their chicken business grew sufficiently. The 500 birds Loren fed daily were among 7,000 his family then raised each year.

But the dream failed. When he was five, the family was forced to put the farm up for sale. Loren hid the for-sale sign in the woods, thinking it would stop the transaction. It didn't, of course.

His mother's brother, Bernard Hambleton, offered the penniless family employment at the psychiatric sanitarium he and his wife, Marion, owned near Seattle. He also gave them lodging in a tiny house on the grounds. Loren and his older brother bedded down on two small beds in one of the rooms and his parents slept on a fold-out sofa in the other. His father was the maintenance man, his mother an aide and cook. The family also did what they knew: they began raising chickens on contract in coops scattered through the region. As a first-grader, Loren was responsible for 3,000 chickens; the number doubled when he was in third grade. By junior high school, his flock grew to 45,000 chickens when his father became too ill to work.

But it wasn't the poultry that Loren would remember decades later. Even now, he has only to close his eyes and he senses the sting in his nose, throat and lungs from waste piled three feet high in the chicken houses. The ache returns to his shoulders and back from hauling tons of the smelly matter out of the coops in an aluminum wheelbarrow during seasonal cleanings.

For years, the failure of the family farm hung over Loren's father like the scent in those chicken houses. Anguish seared ulcers in his abdomen. On some days, he was unable to rise from his bed to go to work. When Loren was 15 and old enough for the responsibility, he took on the job of gofer at the sanitarium. It was there that he witnessed an event he would often talk about later in life: a horse rousing a woman from deep catatonia.

Bernard Hambleton and his wife Marion had purchased Fairfax Hospital from their relatives, Arthur and Caroline Hughes. The couple founded the hospital in Seattle three decades earlier, striking out on their own after working as psychiatric aides. They located the sanitarium in a large frame house on Queen Anne Hill and named it after a local street. Fairfax Hospital's staff quickly grew to include three of the five practicing psychiatrists in the city and a bevy of nurses and aides. In 1936, the Hughes placed a portable structure beside the house to accommodate more patients. About a year later, the city informed the Hughes that they were violating local ordinances. Psychiatric hospitals were not permitted within the city limits.

The couple responded by purchasing a former estate across Lake Washington in Kirkland, which was a rural area then. They had the portable building rolled down the hill, loaded onto a barge, and floated to their new property, where they relocated all of the hospital's operations. The expansive grounds provided an abundance of attributes the Hughes felt were important in the care of the mentally ill: animals, fresh air, lots of room for outdoor activities. By the time Loren's family moved onto the grounds of Fairfax Hospital, the Hughes had retired and sold it to Bernard and Marion Hambleton.

When the Hambletons hired Loren, they assigned him work that was familiar. He helped care for animals, raked leaves, pulled weeds, cleaned. Much of it was reminiscent of life on the farm.

But they also gave him a duty that was new: serving as a companion for the patients. The experts at Fairfax Hospital believed that productive work was important in the treatment of a wide variety of psychiatric disorders. Loren was often told to ask patients to work with him while he went about his duties at the hospital.

It was not unusual for Loren to drive the hospital's truck along twisting roads to the feed store with a 30-year-old man suffering from suicidal tendencies sitting next to him. When the teen received orders to wax the hospital's entire first floor, his helpmate was a stocky heir to an old New England family, under treatment for explosive rages.

Loren never had been trained on patient care. The staff assumed he would figure it out and he did. Adopting a nonchalant and friendly tone, he would invite his charges to "help me out with some stuff today." He learned the art of watching without being noticed, of hearing unvoiced thoughts, desires, and anger.

"If you could understand what the patients were saying with their eyes, the way they held their bodies, you could anticipate what they were about to do, even if they didn't say a word," Loren said decades later.

Loren's weekends differed from the weekdays only in that he didn't go to school. There was always work to do, and he added to the load by starting a veal business with several classmates. Yet he found time for sports. Despite his family's troubles with money, time, and his father's poor health, his parents always encouraged him as an athlete from his first days in Little League through college. He feels now it was a demonstration of their great love for him that was never voiced or even hinted at verbally by his taciturn dad. Loren played football, baseball and basketball, but he was especially drawn to track, the sport where a youth whose life was regulated by an unrelenting schedule of responsibility could run fast.

As Loren neared adulthood, he was sprinting in other ways: he was going to make something of himself. For a long time, he thought it would be as a cattle rancher. He threw himself into preparing for this endeavor, doing hard summer work at Glacier View Ranch, a cattle farm owned by his Uncle Bernard and Aunt Marion, immersing himself in every article he could find on the subject.

By the end of high school, however, the obstacles to his dream became apparent. Farmers in the area were struggling to survive, an ominous harbinger of what would lie ahead for even the most ambitious rancher. He read that starting a cattle ranch required a half-million dollar investment. No matter how many hours he worked at his various jobs, reaching that amount appeared impossible.

When his uncle suggested he use his experience at the sanitarium as the basis of a career as a psychiatric hospital administrator, Loren decided to follow that advice. He pursued a business degree, first at a community college and then at the University of Washington. Besides carrying a full course schedule, he worked as many as 40 hours a week at Fairfax Hospital. He bought out his friends' stakes in the veal business, shouldering its entire workload and he also started raising purebred Black Angus cattle.

In 1972, when Loren was a junior at the university, the Hambletons decided to retire. They sold Fairfax Hospital to Community Psychiatric Centers, a company that operated psychiatric hospitals in several states. A variety of corporate brass with the firm, known as CPC, visited Fairfax Hospital during the transition to the new ownership. Loren had the job of picking up the executives at the airport. One day, while at the wheel, he told the CEO that he planned a career in psychiatric hospital administration. The CEO offered Loren a position as assistant administrator at one of its California hospitals when he graduated.

A year later, Loren arrived at CPC's headquarters for its administrator training program. A vice president emerged from a corner office and told him he was being sent to the purchasing department. Loren refused to be reassigned. After a tense stand-off, the executive yielded and Loren joined the training program alongside two new hires who were 15 years his senior and had worked as administrators elsewhere. Several weeks into the course, a grueling regimen that Loren recalls as "fear-based," he was told he was ready for the job. The others had failed.

Loren was only 22 years of age, fresh-faced and lean. Many made the mistake of assuming Loren was the overgrown kid he appeared to be. But after six months as an assistant administrator, Loren was promoted to an administrator's position at a larger CPC hospital. It was riddled with operational and procedural problems that were resolved once he took the helm.

For years after that assignment, Loren was dispatched to head up the hospitals where CPC had the most problems: census had fallen, staff members were flouting procedures, and adolescent patients were out of control. Invariably, he turned the facilities around.

"I think I've always had the gift of command presence," Loren said many years later. "It's something that works well with animals and when I was growing up, I always did well with bulls. When you have a big animal like that and it isn't happy with you, you need to be able to handle it or you're going to have a problem. At first in these hospitals the staff would doubt me. Once I could get them to cooperate, they would see that what I was doing worked."

Likely, those hospital staffers never met anyone who worked the way Loren did. He grew up never having a day off. It was no different now. When Loren took on a new hospital, he slept there most nights before relocating his family to the area. He lived alongside the patients, the same way he had at Fairfax Hospital. Schizophrenics, the profoundly depressed, the phobia-ridden – they were his fellow residents. So were elders with ebbing memories and unpredictable moods, diagnosed as having Alzheimer's disease or other dementias.

He never considered, and never would, that psychiatric patients were anything other than human beings who happen to have illnesses of the mind. His purpose in living among them went beyond bringing that hospital in line with CPC's rulebook. He was there to raise it to the best level of care.

Loren did not stop running during his years with CPC. He always became bored once he fixed the problem assigned to him. For Loren, it was natural to fill the time with more work, even if he had to create it himself. He developed new programs in marketing and patient care. He attended two independent study graduate programs in hospital administration. One was at Canada's University of Saskatchewan in Saskatoon, because Loren wanted to learn the intricacies of Canada's health care system. The other program was at the University of Minnesota. He also taught himself the ins and outs of property acquisition and hospital development. He pushed CPC's brass hard to expand the company.

Ultimately, Loren charged all the way to the top of the corporate ladder and became president and chief operating officer of CPC's worldwide operations. The firm, which had six mental health hospitals when Loren joined it, grew to operate 50 psychiatric hospitals, over 100 renal dialysis units and it started a sub-acute medical surgical hospital business during his tenure.

Loren's career at CPC spanned two decades. He was in his early twenties and newly married when he began there and a father in his forties when he left. When asked why he walked away from the top post at a successful company, he responds by saying, "The psychiatric industry was changing. Due to the influence of some less-than-ethical operators in the industry, managed care was given free rein to reduce cost, which in large part was done by denying care. I called it the 1-800-JUST SAY NO line."

VASCULAR DEMENTIA

Vascular dementia is widely considered the second most common type of dementia.
See silveradostory.com/vascular

After a few years of this new direction, he believed the trend would not alter. While he was proud of CPC's operations, he didn't want to be part of the industry anymore.

When people make major changes in their lives, they often say it's because the world around them no longer is the same. They don't recognize that the transformation is really within them. People who knew Loren during his career at CPC describe him tactfully as "probably more hard-nosed and aggressive in his focus than he is now." He likely presented that image when he left CPC in 1993, although he had no fixed plans for what to do next.

But doing nothing was unthinkable for the man who worked every day since childhood. He also couldn't shut the door and walk away from those he had assisted, befriended, lived with for so long. And now Loren understood that one group among them needed him

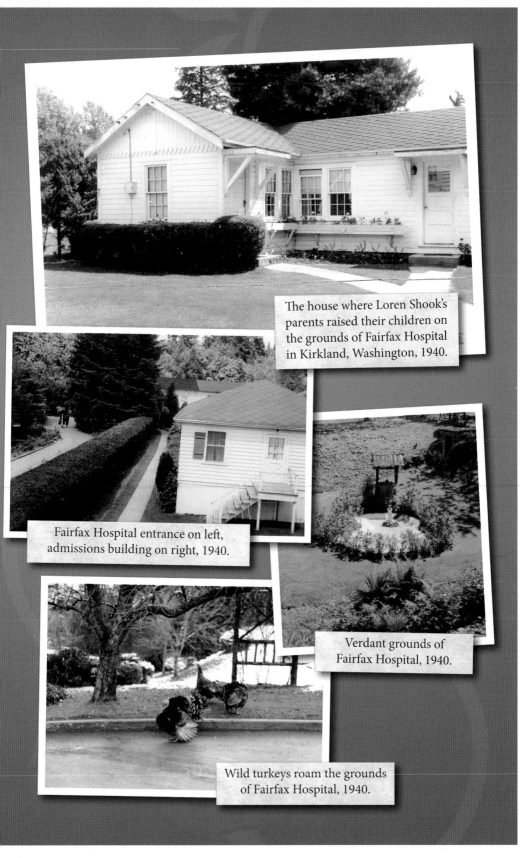

The house where Loren Shook's parents raised their children on the grounds of Fairfax Hospital in Kirkland, Washington, 1940.

Fairfax Hospital entrance on left, admissions building on right, 1940.

Verdant grounds of Fairfax Hospital, 1940.

Wild turkeys roam the grounds of Fairfax Hospital, 1940.

Loren Shook as a young boy, 1958.

Loren's aunt and uncle, Marion and Bernard Hambleton, outside their home in Hawthorne, CA in 1943, prior to moving to Washington to assume operations of Fairfax Hospital, 1946.

Kathleen Shook, Loren's mother, in the kitchen of Fairfax Hospital, 1950.

Fairfax Hospital grounds
after a snowfall, 1940s.

Loren's aunt, Marion
Hambleton, at work in the
Fairfax Hospital admissions
office, 1954.

Fairfax Hospital recreation
building, 1965.

Interior of the recreation building, Fairfax Hospital, 1965.

Main house at Glacier View Ranch near Rockport in Northern Washington, where Loren worked during the summer as a young man.

Heidi the Palomino with friend, Kathy, on the Fairfax Hospital grounds, 1968.

ARCHITECT'S DRAWING OF NEW PSYCHIATRIC TREATMENT CENTER IN JUANITA
Original Hospital Was Floated and Towed Across Lake From Seattle

Fairfax Psychiatric Hospital opens

Fairfax Psychiatric Hospital at 10218 N. E. 132nd St. is a blending of old and new.

The new is a modern psychiatric treatment center that was opened Sunday for public viewing. The old is the original Fairfax Hospital building on Queen Anne Hill that was "floated and towed" across Lake Washington in 1934.

The hospital was founded in 1929 and was incorporated in 1957. Mr. and Mrs. Bernard Hambleton, owners, have operated the hospital since 1950.

* * *

LOCATED in a countrylike atmosphere, the hospital is on approximately 30 acres where some patients are able to ride horseback. The new facility is one-story with both open and closed door accommodations. Included is a large lounge and recreational area and occupational therapy space with a full-time therapist.

Bed capacity at the present time is 80 beds with space to expand to 99 as needed. Both male and female patients are admitted with no age limit. Admissions may be voluntary or by commitment. All patients are under the care of a physician or psychiatrist.

The older portion of the hospital is planned to be used as a geriatric center for care of the aged. It will have a 32 bed capacity.

Frederick Lemere, M.D., is medical director of the hospital.

Hambleton, administrator, is a member of the American College of Hospital Administrators. He has had four years experience as assistant administrator and 17 years as administrator.

Marian Hambleton, R. N., is director of nursing. She received her bachelor of science degree in nursing from the University of Washington and has had eight years experience as a staff nurse and 13 years experience as director of nursing.

The medical staff consists of 36 physicians, including psychiatrists, general practitioners, internists. The staff is organized in accordance with standards of the Joint Commission on Accreditation of Hospitals.

* * *

Personnel includes a nursing staff of 25, including registered nurses, practical nurses and nurses aids. Total personnel is 42.

The hospital is licensed by the State Department of Health of Washington, approved by Medicare and is a member of the American Hospital Association, Washington State Hospital Association and the National Association of Private Psychiatric Hospitals.

Types of care given include psychotherapy, psychoanalysis, electroshock therapy, sub- coma-insula therapy, occupational therapy and recreational therapy.

* * *

TYPES OF patients include extreme senility, acute treatment, outpatients, night care, custodial care, rehabilitation, day care, dope addiction "drying out", LSD patients, alcoholics, and in-patient.

The new Fairfax Psychiatric Hospital was designed and built through the efforts of Mr. and Mrs. Hambleton, Willis McClarty, architect; Gene E. Lyon consultant and builder, and William R. Hanson, construction engineer.

Others contributing were Harry Broman and Ira Cummins, architects for Washington State Health Department; Miss Helen Levitt, Washington State Nursing Consultant to Psychiatric Care Facilities; Mr. Besse, Washington State Sanitarium; Clarence Ross, assistant Washington State Fire Marshal; Dr. A. B. Price, head of the planning and construction section of the Washington State Department of Health.

Construction was by Careage Construction Corp. at a cost of $750,000.

Seattle newspaper clipping announcing the opening of Fairfax Hospital's "new" treatment center, 1968.

Loren's Uncle Bernard and Aunt Marion at Glacier View Ranch, 1994.

Loren with his Uncle Bernard at Glacier View Ranch, 1994.

Loren atop Mt. Ranier, 1969.

Suzanne and Loren Shook, 2010.

Steve Winner at a group home in Chesterfield County, VA, 1976.

Steve as an infant with his mother Frances and sister Cheri.

Steve and Deanelle Winner, 1985.

Steve skiing at Lake Tahoe, 1995.

Silverado Senior Living founders, the late
Jim Smith, Steve Winner and Loren Shook.

Steve presenting the Halloween costume awards at Silverado Senior Living Escondido with nurse Dena, 1998.

Steve pictured with his daughter, Elizabeth and grandson, Ian.

Steve sits with a family member and resident at Silverado Senior Living-Escondido where he served as Administrator in the company's early days.

Silverado Licensed Vocational Nurse, April, and her daughter, Sarah, enjoy listening to a resident play the violin at Silverado Senior Living – The Huntington.

Residents and an associate petting the miniature horses at Silverado Senior Living Encinitas.

Silverado Chaplain David Pascoe with a Silverado Hospice patient, Salt Lake City, UT.

Silverado Senior Living-Newport Mesa resident Rose Arrington won a gold medal in a softball throwing contest at the age of 100.

Rose Arrington appears on Times Square Jumbotron, 2008.

Silverado's unique "memory boxes" captivate residents, family members and associates.

Intergenerational activities are important for the memory-impaired. Here a resident helps to feed the child of a Silverado associate.

A resident helps prepare a delicious meal at Silverado Senior Living-Turtle Creek in Dallas.

Andrea engages in a game of bingo with residents at Silverado Senior Living-San Juan Capistrano.

A Service Club member from Silverado Senior Living-Newport Mesa helps to teach a class of seniors at an adult day services center how to prepare a potted plant.

Silverado resident Walter, 99, and his friend, Lisa, 7, greet one of the community pets at Silverado Senior Living-Escondido.

the most. They were the people with Alzheimer's disease, vascular dementia, Parkinson's, and other conditions that robbed memory.

Psychiatric hospitals weren't the right place for them, Loren realized. They were not mentally ill. They had diseases of the brain which produced symptoms that at times appeared psychiatric in nature, but were actually biological. With rare exceptions, their conditions developed after six or seven robust decades building families, careers, friendships, avocations, routines. Now,

PARKINSON'S DISEASE

Parkinson's disease (PD) is a degenerative neurological disorder of the brain related to a depletion of a neurotransmitter called dopamine.
See silveradostory.com /parkinsons

they had lost everything they loved and the world had become an alien place. But those hospitals, or nursing homes whose grimness appalled Loren when his father needed services for a non-operable brain tumor that caused severe dementia-like symptoms in his later years, were the only options for their care.

Every experience in Loren's life had built up to this moment. After CPC, Loren spent several years preparing to risk everything he had to save these people.

Chapter Six
Two Minds, One Vision

Vision is the art of seeing what is invisible to others.

Jonathan Swift

O f all the experts who stepped up to the podium at the symposium that day, only one was a layperson. Yet he drew the largest crowd.

Physicians, nurses, social workers, and psychologists filled the room. Many leaned against the walls to hear Steve Winner, a revolutionary in Alzheimer's care. He told the audience:

"Get the memory-impaired up, dressed, and out of their rooms first thing in the morning.

Untie the straps and belts that confine their bodies. Stop giving the drugs that dull their psyches.

Ban block-stacking and balloon toss and other childish pastimes. Fill their days with art classes, music jams, and other activities that matter.

Haul away the vinyl couches, the linoleum tables, the metal seats. Move in fabric sofas, overstuffed chairs, colorful curtains and paintings.

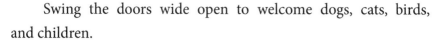

Swing the doors wide open to welcome dogs, cats, birds, and children.

Cheer as these people come back to life."

When Steve finished, those in attendance at the University of California at San Diego's 1995 Alzheimer's Symposium stood to roar their approval. Dozens of them swarmed toward him with questions.

One man sat writing page after page of notes. He stayed seated long after Steve had finished, his expression pensive.

Loren had never met Steve before. He hadn't even heard of him. But what he just witnessed was a vista opening wide in front of him after a long search. After leaving CPC, Loren had decided to learn all he could about Alzheimer's disease and other types of dementia. He wanted to open a different place than those he had seen for people with memory impairment. It would be somewhere they could really *live.* All those years he had been on this quest, he never knew there was someone else out there who thought the way he did.

As it happened, Steve was not an obvious candidate as an Alzheimer's rebel. In his youth, he had just a fleeting brush with memory impairment. An aunt developed Alzheimer's disease and moved into a nursing home. Steve visited her from time to time to break her daily routine of doing nothing. Only much later did Steve understand how stultifying her last years had been. The thought pained him.

Steve entered the University of Maryland planning to major in business. Soon after arriving, he started looking for a job to help pay his college expenses. He spotted an ad for a part-time position as a caregiver in a group home for the mentally disabled. It called for the employee to work weekends, sleeping at the group home on Friday and Saturday nights. He was hired. The position would leave weekdays free to attend classes and study.

His first evening on the job, Steve made sure all of the residents had turned in and then he retired to the staff bedroom. Noise jolted him awake and upright in the early hours of the morning. Voices were coming from the downstairs living room. They were rising and falling with vehemence. Steve pulled on his bathrobe and padded down the steps to find out why so many residents had left their beds.

"When I walked into the room, I discovered just one person was there," Steve recalled. "He was talking in eight different voices."

Steve had not been trained on how to handle such a situation. He took a deep breath and went with his instincts. "Come on, William," he said gently. "It's really time for you to be asleep."

William nodded, stood up from the sofa, and allowed Steve to walk him back upstairs to his room.

The experience got Steve off to an awkward start. For the first few weeks, he continued to feel uncomfortable around the residents. But then, as he lived among them over time and heard their life stories, he began seeing them as individuals.

Lois, for example, had only stubble on her scalp when she moved into the home. She came from a large state-run institution where she had been exiled as a child. It was standard practice there to shave everyone's head.

And something more had been done to Lois, something that could never be made right. She was forcibly sterilized during her teen years, destroying her dream of having a family.

Steve never forgot how Lois talked about this trauma, how she alternately sobbed and raged over it. Lois could have been any woman struggling to come to terms with a very personal tragedy. Indeed, Steve saw that Lois was like any woman. Her mental disability did not make her less than female, less than human. It was simply part of Lois as an individual.

Over the next few years, Steve watched Lois blossom. She grew her hair to her shoulders. She got a job, moved into an apartment, fell in love, married.

Steve fell in love, too, albeit in a different way. He discovered that he was drawn to these people, to connecting with their dreams, thoughts, and talents. Helping the mentally disabled carve their places in the world, building lives filled with purpose and pleasure, mattered. He discarded business as a career and declared his major in behavioral psychology.

Upon graduating from college, he turned his passion into his career. He landed a position directing programs for the developmentally disabled in Virginia. At the same time, he began studying for a master's degree in rehabilitative counseling. He started his coursework with a two-week session on normalization at Syracuse University led by one of its pioneers, Dr. Wolf Wolfensberger. It was there that Steve began to consider what he had learned at the group home in a greater context. He listened raptly as Dr. Wolfensberger and other professors talked of how society identifies groups of people as apart from the norm and considers them of less value. This can lead to humiliation, mistreatment, deprivation of their rights, even of their right to live.

"Those two weeks changed me in a very fundamental way," Steve says decades later. "Once you understand these principles, you never see things the same, whether you are looking at social practices or political situations."

As part of his studies, he visited large state institutions for the mentally handicapped to collect research for Dr. Wolfensberger. Steve had heard about these places from Lois and other residents at the group home, where they had come as an early wave in the movement to bring the mentally handicapped into the mainstream of life. But hearing about them didn't prepare him for seeing them.

"They were horror shows."

Long afterwards, what he witnessed remained sharp in his memory. "The staff would unlock these big heavy double doors and you would walk through into the wards. You would find the people there half-naked, sometimes sitting in their feces. They would be crying, yelling, rocking and no one was paying any attention. I was in shock that human beings could be treated this way."

The normalization theory of Bengt Nirje and Dr. Wolfensberger became Steve's holy grail. Living in the group home, Steve had quickly come to regard those around him as people, rather than as social outcasts. Now, he understood the continuing peril they would be in until society as a whole embraced them. He vowed he would do all he could to change social attitudes.

In 1980, Steve moved to southern California, where he became program director for the developmentally disabled and psychiatric wings of Georgian Court, a health care facility. Georgian Court changed hands several years later and the new owners converted it to a geriatric care center. Steve never planned to work in geriatrics, but he needed time. He stayed on at Georgian Court and trained for a license as a nursing home administrator while he searched for a job in his field.

It was difficult. He recoiled at how Georgian Court cared for its residents. They were kept clean and fed; their medications were given as needed. But the staff barely knew their names, let alone anything about them as people. The patients spent their days tied into wheelchairs lining Georgian Court's hallways, backs to the wall and eyes looking blankly into space.

"Couldn't we at least turn the wheelchairs so that people face each other, so they have eye contact, maybe even talk to each other?" Steve asked at a management meeting. The executives blinked, baffled. Their puzzlement soon turned to irritation as the young interloper offered more ideas in subsequent gatherings. After six months, Steve left Georgian Court. He was hired to direct a large organization of residences and rehabilitation programs for the mentally disabled.

Three years passed. Then the work that Steve turned away from, that he never thought he would do, tapped him on the shoulder. Or rather, it came in a phone call. The previous owner of Georgian Court was on the line. He now worked for a company planning to convert a skilled nursing facility into a place dedicated to Alzheimer's care. Parkside Special Care Center for the memory-impaired would be the first of its kind in Southern California. If Steve were interested in becoming its administrator, the company would pay for him to visit Alzheimer's care centers around the country. Then he could design his own program for Parkside.

At first, Steve dismissed the idea. Working with the developmentally disabled was the career he had trained for, that stirred his passions.

But he had trouble putting the offer out of his mind. He always felt regret for the elderly residents he had left behind at Georgian Court. He had been powerless to help them. This call out of the blue was a chance to make things right, if not for the people at Georgian Court, at least for others facing a similar plight.

He took the job.

When Steve embarked on his first round of visits to Alzheimer's care facilities across the United States, he assumed he would return with pages of notes on practices to emulate. He was counting on it, since he had no experience in that area.

But his notepad remained empty even after the last of his journeys. The facilities he saw shocked him. He might have been walking the halls of Georgian Court once again. There were the same rows of wheelchairs along hallways, the same lifeless stares by seniors lost in inactivity and anonymity. If these places were the gold standard in memory care, they would have to change, or rather, Steve was going to change them.

Steve's field, developmental disability care, was the only one using the principles and practices of normalization, but Steve believed they would serve equally well in Alzheimer's care. After all, the memory-impaired confined to those unfeeling nursing homes lost their social status just as the mentally disabled had. They were exiled outside of the normality of the world, which considered them less than human.

Steve would transform care for the memory-impaired by restoring their normal.

Parkside Special Care Center had tile floors, vinyl-covered furniture bolted to the floor, employees in white uniforms, and countless televisions blaring non-stop in front of motionless residents. Reshaping Parkside to Steve's vision would be a Herculean task. Everything about the place needed change, including the attitudes of the staff. Not all of them would stay, Steve was sure.

Making a transformation of this magnitude is overwhelming. It's best to take a cue from the old saw about how to eat an elephant: Just do it one bite at a time.

So when Steve arrived at Parkside for his first day on the job, his golden retriever Jasper was at his side. Key to transforming Parkside would be having everyone on the same page. They needed to understand it was not a facility for the memory-impaired; it was their home. And there's nothing more normal than having a dog around the house.

While pet therapy would become an accepted practice in senior care in subsequent decades, it was unheard of when Jasper trotted into the front hallway. Animals were considered a sanitation hazard. This was the kind of thing that could push the eyebrows of state inspectors sky high. But if Steve were going to bust standards in the

> ### PET THERAPY
>
> *Several studies have shown health benefits of people's interaction with pets both mentally and physically. The pets at Silverado communities offer unconditional love to all residents. See silveradostory.com/pets*

interests of those in his care, he wasn't going to worry about what they thought. He was more immediately concerned about the staff.

Lori had been working in Parkside's medical records department for two years before Steve's arrival.

"Steve had a totally different vision of what Parkside should be, what it could be, and we took it as an insult to what we had been doing," she said.

In meeting after meeting, Steve laid out his ideas to the incredulous employees. The floors would be redone in a pattern the residents could follow. It would encourage them to walk. Colorful wallpaper, plush furniture, and leafy plants would turn the atmosphere from clinical to inviting. More dogs and cats would join Jasper, along with tanks of fish and cages of birds.

Staff would keep the doors of the offices open. "If residents wander in, invite them to sit down," Steve said. "Your office is a room in their home. They have as much right to go there as you do."

Residents would wear regular clothing during the day, rather than bathrobes and slippers. "We will need to call their families and ask them to bring in more of their clothes."

All beds would be made by 9:30 a.m., "because it's not normal to leave a bed unmade until the afternoon." Steve would pitch in to help and so should other managers if it looked like the deadline might not be met.

"And unless the residents are choosing to watch television, turn the TVs off and get people involved in something meaningful."

The changes Steve planned alarmed Pat, the activities director. She trained diligently for her work; she prided herself on it. Steve could see Pat was upset. They sat down for a private conversation.

"Pat, think about what you like to do with your friends," Steve said. "When you get together, do you toss balloons? Do you stack blocks? Do you look at calendars and remind each other what the date is?" That last practice, a well-intentioned effort to reorient the memory-impaired to reality, simply causes confusion and stress, Steve explained. And how important is it that any of us knows today's date?

She was silent for a few minutes. Pat had never considered this idea before. She had to admit it made sense, but it contradicted everything she had been taught. This was a different approach and

Steve was asking that Pat design the new activities program herself. The prospect of failure terrified her. "I resigned three times in the first six months, but Steve always told me I couldn't leave, that the residents needed me, that he needed me."

Soon, Parkside began to offer a program of activities unprecedented for those with memory impairment. Groups formed for residents to enjoy music, art, travel, movies. Male residents were invited to put on ties and take part in men's club. Steve used his own money to buy ties for men who didn't have them.

Many employees left.

"Those who stayed discovered new meaning in their work," Lori, the medical records staffer, said. "When you finally understood what Steve was doing, you had more compassion. You realized that before, the people being cared for at Parkside were patients. They weren't individuals that you got to know. And you saw that when you gave them the opportunity to achieve more, to do more, they did it."

Each day brought a gratifying surprise. Staff discovered that many residents considered incontinent were not. They required assistance getting to the restroom and they no longer had the verbal skills to ask for help. But they communicated their need through body language. Once staff identified its meaning, it was easy to understand and to escort them to the bathroom when needed. Liberation from the humiliating lack of continence was a powerful tonic for these residents.

Steve constantly had to persuade state inspectors that Parkside wasn't breaking rules; it was setting new standards of care. In less than a year, Parkside was transformed from a nursing home like any other into a place that families wanted their memory-impaired loved ones to reside. A waiting list developed. Within three years, Parkside's owners purchased a second nursing home for Steve to transform and manage.

Alzheimer's care experts from around the country visited. They wanted to see this revolution for themselves. Conference organizers around the country sought Steve as a speaker. He appeared at the White House Conference on Aging. When Steve stepped up to the podium in front of the audience that included Loren, he had been leading this movement for a decade.

———————

In the three years prior to taking his seat at Steve's presentation, Loren had spent nearly all his waking hours finding out all he could about Alzheimer's care. He visited facilities with memory-impairment units, read every medical journal he could locate, peppered leaders in the field with questions. He was planning to start an organization dedicated to caring for people with memory disorders and he wanted to learn from the best.

The odyssey was frustrating. Those facilities turned out to be nothing more than the usual nursing-home style establishments, "stinky places that felt like warehouses, where the managers would count the peas on residents' plates to make sure they weren't exceeding their budgets," Loren remembered.

The articles and the experts disappointed him, too. They saw the memory-impaired as afflicted, incapacitated, cases without hope. Loren knew them as people with interests, desires, potential.

What he saw, what he heard: He wanted to liberate the memory-impaired from this, not condemn them to it. Loren had enlisted longtime CPC colleague Jim Smith to help with the complex financial and real estate issues involved in launching the company he envisioned. Both men knew the organization would only come to life the way they wanted if they could find the right person to lead resident care. This would be someone who would smile in agreement when Loren talked about providing meaningful lives to people with memory impairment. But everyone they had met so far looked puzzled at best and aghast at worst when Loren described his plans.

Chapter Seven
The Dream Takes Shape

And above all, watch with glittering eyes the whole world around you because the greatest secrets are always hidden in the most unlikely places. Those who don't believe in magic will never find it.

Roald Dahl

He came in with his friend, claiming to be searching for a place to care for his aging mother. She had Alzheimer's disease, he said. Wearing jackets and no ties, they were trying hard to look casual, Steve Winner noticed. As Steve showed the pair around Parkside Special Care Center, they fired questions at him, jotting his answers on pads encased in leather bindings.

Their manner and the depth of their inquiries about Parkside's services didn't square with how people usually talked in this situation. Emotion often overwhelmed the spouses and children of the memory-impaired. Many were still struggling to comprehend basic facts about the disease that was changing their loved one.

When the two men said they wanted also to visit Lo-Har Lodge, the other memory-care center Steve oversaw, it clinched it. Steve guessed they were state inspectors hoping to snag Parkside and Lo-Har in a bureaucratic trap. Regulators had been visiting him to challenge the two centers' unusual memory care programs for years. Steve played along with the ruse.

After he finished escorting the pair around both Parkside and Lo-Har Lodge, the two asked if they could meet with him privately. Steve took a deep breath and got ready for the blow: *Bring it on, State of California. I'm ready.*

He showed them into his office and left the door open. "Parkside is the residents' home," he explained to his visitors. "They can go anywhere they wish, even here. If you don't want anyone to hear us, keep your voices down." Both men made another note as they settled into chairs facing Steve's desk. The man whose mother had Alzheimer's disease – or so he said – leaned forward.

"We're starting an assisted living community for people with memory impairment," Loren said. "We're trying to find the right person to take charge of the resident care and make it everything we want it to be. You're the person we've been looking for. Will you join us?"

Steve drew back in surprise. Then he smiled and said, "Thank you, but I'm happy right here where I am."

Loren leaned in closer. Beside him, Jim Smith sat forward too. Then Loren began to describe his vision of a place that people with memory-impairment would blossom.

Steve had never seen Loren before. He had never heard of him. He sat silently as the stranger voiced Steve's own thoughts, feelings, and dreams. When Loren finished speaking, Steve asked a simple question – the only one that came to mind at that moment.

"Will you have many pets?"

"Yes, we love pets," Loren said. "We're going to have a lot of them."

"How many is a lot?"

"We're not putting any limit on the number and we're going to have every kind of pet you can imagine. But how about if you come work with us and then you can help us with pets?"

All three men laughed. The ice broke. The trio spent several hours comparing ideas and spinning out scenarios. Anyone glancing into Steve's office would have thought these guys were the best of buddies.

"What are you going to call your company?" Steve asked.

"Silverado Senior Living," Loren and Jim told him. It was Loren's idea. He was naming it after the Silverado Resort and Country Club in California's Napa Valley. He went there once with his family. He liked it a lot. The resort offered tennis as well as golf, many amenities, and a whole host of other activities.

"They have something for everyone in the family to enjoy, regardless of their age or interests," Loren said. "That is exactly how it's going to be for the people at our community and for everyone, kids and adults alike, who come to visit."

When Loren and Jim rose to leave, they asked Steve to think about their offer. "Don't decide either way right now. Please just take some time to consider what we discussed."

Steve had no intention of accepting. Nearly a decade had passed since he revolutionized care for people with Alzheimer's disease at Parkside Special Care Center. He had brought the same changes to Lo-Har Lodge four years ago. When he closed his eyes, he could see each one of the hundreds of residents he had known over the years. He remembered the moment an activity, a friendship, the laughter of a child or the warmth of a pet brought them to life. How could he give even a moment's consideration to leaving a place that was part of him?

But in the days that followed, he found himself thinking about the way Loren talked. Steve had never met anyone who had spoken his own mind and sentiments the way Loren did. It was the purest passion.

A few weeks later, Steve fished Loren's card out of his desk and called him. He scheduled an appointment with Loren and Jim at their office in Orange County, California. The three men squeezed their chairs together in the small space and again talked for several hours. Not long after that meeting, "I went with my gut," Steve said. He called Loren and Jim and told them that he would come aboard.

For the next year, Steve held two jobs. He kept his position as administrator at Parkside and Lo-Har Lodge. At night, he worked with Loren and Jim to plan Silverado's resident care program. He told the owners of Parkside and Lo-Har what he was doing. They understood. The man who had designed their revolutionary memory-care programs wanted to stand again before an empty frame and fill it with his vision.

During that time, Silverado existed solely in the minds of the three men. Loren and Jim were searching for a building – perhaps a skilled nursing facility or mental health hospital – to turn into their first memory-care community.

One day, Steve received the call he had been expecting for 12 months: "Give your notice," Loren said. "We've got the place." Steve wrapped up his work at Parkside and Lo-Har Lodge and hugged residents and staff goodbye. Shortly after Steve turned in his keys, Loren called again. The deal had fallen through. Steve spent anxious days regretting what he thought could be the biggest mistake of his life.

Then one afternoon, as Steve was working in Loren and Jim's tiny office, the pair strode in and said the deal was back on. Silverado was taking possession of the property that day. The three of them needed to get there as fast as possible. They piled into Loren's car and headed south from Orange County to where Silverado would take shape: a nursing home in Escondido, California.

"It's a pit," Loren told Steve as he maneuvered through heavy traffic. "It can accommodate 110 people. Right now, there are only 20. It has a bad reputation; it's been through two bankruptcies." Loren described the knee-high weeds sprouting in the backyard. Cracks crisscrossed the floors, lamps languished with burnt-out bulbs, chairs and sofas were so worn that "you'd likely fall through if you actually sat down. And the staff won't look anyone in the eye."

The facility certainly didn't meet the criteria the new owners had set for their dream location, but after months of searching and fruitless negotiations, they felt it was now or never. They would have to make this work.

"At some point, you have to put your primary focus on getting the company going, getting the concepts in place," Loren said later. "You can't wait forever to make things happen."

For Loren, more was riding on this endeavor than just his dream. He had convinced a private equity firm to invest in the project, an impressive feat in an era when venture capitalists were enamored by Internet companies. He and Jim had invested a great deal of their own money and he was also placing personal financial guarantees on his new company. But those around him then say he never displayed anything but certainty.

As the three men headed toward Escondido, the dark clouds overhead opened and unexpected hail began to pound the highway. They pulled under an overpass to wait it out. "I hope this isn't an omen," Steve said, his apprehension apparent behind the joke.

The skies quickly cleared after the sudden storm. When the trio arrived at the nursing home and walked in, its administrator stormed down the hall toward them. She hurled a ring of keys at them as she passed and snarled, "Here, it's all yours now." She slammed her way out the front door. A moment later, they heard a car start and peel out of the parking lot.

Coming into the half-lit lobby from outside, it took a few moments for their eyes to adjust. "Wait, where are the couch and the chairs?" Jim asked. Loren scanned the area. The furniture had vanished. Decrepit as it was, its absence and the semi-darkness made the place ghostly.

Then they heard faint noise from one of the corridors. It was originating behind a door marked "Dining Room." They pushed it open and found residents sitting around linoleum tables. Wraith-like and silent, many were in wheelchairs, their faces turned down to their laps. The sound came from a corner of the room, where an employee was shuffling tableware in a plastic bin.

While some residents were picking at their food, most ignored it. Loren, Jim and Steve approached the tables. The plate in front of each person held several yellowing pieces of lettuce and a small scoop of macaroni salad. Steve drew in his breath sharply. He leaned down beside the resident nearest to him and gently said: "Hi, I'm Steve. Is this all you're having for dinner?" The woman didn't respond. He stood and pushed his way through double doors at the back of the room. They led into the kitchen. A man in a dingy jacket was leaning against a counter.

"What are you serving?" he demanded. "Do you have anything decent for the residents to eat, any meat, anything with flavor?"

In his fury, Steve didn't introduce himself. The man didn't ask who Steve was. "We stopped feeding them meat a long time ago," he said. "The owners ran out of money."

He paused and then added: "We buy stale bread in bulk. A lot of nights, we pour canned gravy over it and serve it to them as meat loaf."

Steve pivoted and strode back to talk with Loren and Jim. This wasn't going to be the first meal at the place under their watch, the three agreed. Loren stayed to keep an eye on the community while Steve and Jim drove to the nearest McDonald's. They bought bagfuls of hamburgers, chicken nuggets, and French fries and brought them back to the residents.

The fragrance emanating from the paper sacks was a powerful elixir. People who had seemed barely awake as they slumped around the tables began stretching their hands out for the food. They smiled, some spoke. Despite the sorry surroundings, the meal took on the air of a picnic.

Steve arranged to bring supplies from Parkside Special Care Center to tide the residents over until he could order what was needed. He had left on excellent terms; the owners were happy to help.

Something else that came from Parkside and stayed was a team of long-time employees who were eager to assist Steve in shaping this new venture.

"There was nothing I wouldn't do for him," said Lori, the medical records staffer at Parkside. This included learning how to cook. The job of chef was the only position available to her in Silverado's early days. Lori sought recipes from her mother and multiplied the serving quantity by 10. Her cinnamon rolls became a resident favorite. But she still blushes over the morning she overcooked the eggs and they turned green. "Everyone was nice about it, but nobody

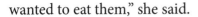

wanted to eat them," she said.

She taught herself how to operate all of the kitchen equipment. According to the business plan drawn up by Loren and Jim, occupancy would need to reach 40 residents before Silverado could afford to hire a dishwasher. In the meantime, Lori handled that task, as well.

While Steve and the employees focused on resident care, Loren and Jim set about renovating the place. Comfortable furniture, colorful paint and wallpaper, and sparkling cleanliness were priorities. So were flowers, walking paths, and a playground for visiting youngsters. A source of special pride was the chandelier they installed in the dining room. The dreary room became an inviting centerpiece, where people lingered after meals to talk. Even Loren, Jim, and Steve were surprised when seven residents who once needed assistance at mealtime began to eat on their own, from the sheer pleasure and energy of being in that room.

Ben was Silverado's first official new resident. Husky and over six feet tall, he had lost little of the strength that powered his college football career decades earlier. Ben came to Silverado from the hospital, where he had angrily assaulted nurses and orderlies. For that reason, his hands and feet were tied down to the gurney that rolled him into the community. His wife walked behind him, weeping. Silverado agreed to accept Ben in spite of his violence. If he lashed out here and hurt someone, she wouldn't know where to turn next because no other senior living community would take him, she told Steve. He did his best to reassure her: Silverado was Ben's home now. Let's focus on getting him well.

Steve and the staff were certain from reviewing Ben's history and observing him that he was in physical pain. No longer able to communicate through words in a way those around him could understand, he was expressing his anguish through punches and kicks. The abundance of psychotropic drugs being put into his body was aggravating his condition.

The Silverado staff freed Ben from his restraints. They placed a mattress on the floor for him so he wouldn't fall far should he move from his bed. They adjusted Ben's pain medication and cut back on other drugs. Then they introduced him to Cassie, the community's resident Labrador retriever. Steve still smiles as he recalls the delicate dance between the two. At first, Cassie would walk up to Ben as he reclined on his bed and push her muzzle into his palms. Ben pulled back. Then one day, he reached out a hand and petted her. When he stopped, she thrust her head at him to ask for more. He turned away.

But a few days later, when Cassie wanted a second round of attention, Ben responded. At about this time, Ben began to smile. He defied the doctors who said he would never walk again. He could sleep in a regular bed and sit comfortably in a chair. He became the Ben his family and friends had loved, a cheerful man who made it his responsibility to welcome visitors and newcomers to the community with Cassie by his side.

What was happening at Silverado got noticed. New residents began to arrive regularly after Ben moved in. A waiting list developed. Lori, there from the beginning, wasn't surprised. "When you heard Loren speak about our vision, that we were there to provide the best memory care in the world, no one would doubt for a moment what we were doing and that it would succeed."

Chapter Eight
Insist on Great Care

Love will find a way through paths where wolves fear to prey.

Lord Byron

People don't know what they don't know.

"If more families knew what's possible in memory care -- that it can be great -- they would demand it for their loved ones instead of settling for the most acceptable option they can find in their town. Their call for superb care would improve the lives of the memory-impaired everywhere," Loren Shook insists.

After a decade and a half of operation, Silverado has the statistics that prove what outstanding care can achieve. By 2010, over 3,300 memory-impaired people who couldn't walk when they came to Silverado had begun to walk again. More than 2,400 of those unable to eat on their own regained that ability. Seven hundred residents started to attend to their own toileting needs.

Silverado reduces the number of medications the memory-impaired take each day by as much as 50 percent. Residents' physical and mental health improves as a result.

Should a person in Silverado's care fall, chances are about one percent that he or she will fracture a bone. This figure is far below the six to eight percent national rate of fractures from falls by the frail elderly.

The numbers give quantitative proof of Silverado's success. But Silverado doesn't keep these records for bragging rights. Loren says, "Our intention is to raise the quality of care for the memory-impaired, not just at Silverado, but around the globe. We record this information and make it public to give families a benchmark they can use to hold providers to a higher standard."

Loren explains how this record-keeping began. At first, the staff at Silverado's sole location in Escondido, California maintained handwritten notes on several topics, such as ambulation, feeding, weight, hospitalizations, falls among residents. As Silverado grew into other areas, the data widened, too. Now, computerized statistics provide real-time data on everything from medication types and frequency to pressure wounds, empowering the Silverado leader with relevant and measurable clinical outcome data serving a unique population. This kind of data is not available anywhere else.

Regulations mandate that skilled nursing facilities collect data on their patients. Those requirements don't apply to Silverado as an assisted living organization. It voluntarily records this information for its own use and encourages all providers to record data and share it openly. Unfortunately, for the most part, the call has gone unheeded.

"If all of us in the field of memory-care worked together on this issue, it would have a huge impact on the well-being of the memory-impaired everywhere," Loren noted. "This is one of the single biggest steps we could collectively take to benefit millions of people."

Loren and Steve witness Silverado's impact every day. Silverado has expanded greatly since its founding. It now offers the continuum of care, including the home care and care management services of Silverado At Home, multiple Silverado Senior Living memory-care communities and Silverado Hospice. But the pair continues to visit all of Silverado's locations constantly. It's not uncommon to see Loren chatting with a gentleman in the bistro of one of the communities or Steve walking arm-in-arm with a lady on a flowered path outside. They have never lost the exhilaration that comes of seeing a life changed for the better.

At the foundation of Silverado's practices is an emotion that is sorely lacking in healthcare today. That emotion is love. And it's not just about feeling love; it's about expressing it. Loren has provided the theme for this concept which has always been fundamental to Silverado: *Love is Greater than Fear.* This principle guides Silverado's operations. From this tenet, nurses, caregivers, and all other staff know they should base their actions on what is in the best interest of those they serve, whether as residents and patients, family members, or other employees. They never need to feel afraid to demonstrate love through words, actions, or hugs.

An important aspect of the *Love is Greater than Fear* principle is Silverado's commitment to providing the memory-impaired with an environment where they can succeed. For those living with deteriorating memory in the world outside of Silverado, each day brings corrections, reminders, and rebukes that emphasize their missteps.

"You already had breakfast."

"You've said that same thing five times today."

"You can't come with us. We won't be able to handle you."

The litany chips away at their self-esteem, blighting their spirits.

Even as their cognitive function ebbs, they nonetheless understand that they are now regarded as an embarrassment. Their physical and mental well-being declines. They find it's easier not to speak, not to try to participate. It's easier to stay in bed than risk further rejection.

But at Silverado, those with memory-impairment and those without belong to the same community. Residents aren't told they're wrong. They're in a place where the answer is yes.

"You're still hungry for some more breakfast? Let's go see what we can find that you would like."

"You always make me laugh with that story. Thank you for telling it to me."

"A group of us are going; please come with us!"

"When a person comes into our care, their family usually gives us a list of all the things that person can no longer do," related Anne Ellett, a nurse practitioner with a master's degree in nursing. She is Silverado's senior vice president of health services. "They'll say 'She doesn't walk anymore, she doesn't feed herself, she doesn't want to participate in anything.' We thank them for the information, but we don't take it as the final answer."

At Silverado, a list of apparently lost abilities merely represents a description of how that memory-impaired person seemed in a prior environment, at home or in another senior care community. Silverado conducts its own evaluation, keeping in mind that for the memory-impaired, "It's never one thing that makes a difference in their health. It's a combination of many things."

This approach is crucial, according to Joe W. Ramsdell, M.D., Professor and Division Head, General Internal Medicine at the

University of California, San Diego.

"A lot of behaviors that memory-impaired people develop in less supportive environments may not indicate how they will do at Silverado. A fresh assessment is a true advantage," Dr. Ramsdell said.

New residents are blank canvasses. They, with the help of Silverado, start over to paint a fresh portrait of what they can become.

With the first brush stroke, Silverado examines whether the new resident has received the right diagnosis. The words Alzheimer's and dementia are used interchangeably in the daily lexicon. However, memory-impairment results from a wide range of origins. The symptoms may appear similar at times, but the progression of the conditions, the range of potential behavior and the factors that have an impact, positive or negative, can vary widely. Understanding the nature of the memory-impairing disease provides the platform on which to build an individual's care program.

Silverado also reviews a new resident's medications. More than half of the people who arrive at Silverado for care are taking too many of them. Psychotropic drugs and sedatives are all too often used to cope with so-called behavior problems. Many are also on other kinds of medications that no longer apply to their health.

For example, a person previously prescribed a drug to reduce blood pressure may still be taking it, even though his pressure is now normal. This explains why he has been falling when he stands – his blood pressure is too low to for him to sustain balance. Prior to coming to Silverado, those caring for him solved the problem by tying him to his wheelchair, but they continued to administer his blood pressure pills, which were the real culprit in this instance.

"It's amazing how often things like a medication review can make a dramatic difference in the life and health of the memory-impaired," Dr. Ramsdell said.

Fundamental to Silverado is its assumption that everyone in its care is prone to falling. Restraining them, however, to wheelchairs and beds is not the solution to that problem or beneficial for their overall health. Silverado never uses restraints of any kind, physical or pharmaceutical. Such limitations deny the individual his or her rights. Human beings should have the opportunity to take risks. There is dignity in risk.

Sometimes, family members resist Silverado's practice of liberating their loved one from restraints. The prospect there will be a fall and that an injury will be sustained frightens them. Invariably, they come to understand and celebrate the resident's restored dignity, the ability to be an active and independent person.

Silverado believes everyone can benefit from physical therapy, so each new resident is evaluated and then placed on a physical therapy program. Silverado also looks at other factors that can affect gait and balance, such as shoes and glasses. As soon as possible, new residents who haven't been walking are reintroduced to it. They may start by wearing a gait belt, which allows caregivers to walk beside them with their hand on the belt to provide assistance with balance. Residents may wear hip protectors, padded garments designed to protect them if a fall should occur.

Caring for Silverado's animals, group strolls and many other activities are structured to incorporate walking. Also, Silverado combines walking and healthy nutrition by filling its country kitchens with finger foods, such as small sandwiches and pieces of fruit that hungry residents can snack on while taking a stroll. Below-normal weight is a common problem in the memory-impaired and so rebuilding weight and muscle is important in regaining the ability to walk.

The company's restorative care program accompanies physical therapy. The only one in the country designed specifically for the memory-impaired, it seeks to reintroduce residents to activities of daily life. For instance, hand-over-hand feeding is used for residents who have not been able to handle their own knife and fork for a long time. At each meal, caregivers guide the resident's hand with their own. After a while, the resident relearns the skill of eating with utensils.

Silverado also assesses new residents through a process called Behavior Mapping. During the first three days at a community, caregivers record the resident's behavior every half hour. What is

HAND-OVER-HAND

Hand-over-hand is a technique to help others learn or re-learn a lost activity or skill.
See silveradostory.com/hand

she doing, what is she saying or not saying, what does she seem to like, when does she become hungry? Does she seem drawn to group activities or is she avoiding them? Nurses study the behavior map to find patterns that will guide them in providing the individual's care.

The staff uses the process again if a resident's behavior changes. A departure from normal preferences and patterns may signal an underlying problem that may not be obvious. The person may be in physical pain or confronting an emotional issue, but is unable to express himself through words. Their behavior change is a request for help. Analyzing the map, the care team can usually identify the issue and resolve it.

Silverado's multi-faceted practices have had an impact on memory-impairment care as a whole, Dr. Ramsdell noted.

"A number of approaches that Silverado piloted have since been adopted elsewhere and the overall level of memory care is improving. Still, Silverado remains in a league of its own," he said.

Susan Frazier is project guide for the Green House Project, the national non-profit organization dedicated to creating long-term care environments that are meaningful for living and working. She remains inspired by a visit to Silverado that "rocked my world and opened my eyes to what could be done." In her work for the Green House Project, she consults with senior care communities nationwide, "which allows me to share with them ideas I first saw at Silverado and this greatly benefits residents, families, and staff."

When Rose came to Silverado from a hospital at the age of 100, she was bedridden, unresponsive, suffering from pneumonia and couldn't eat without help. Rose had always been a strong and independent woman. She graduated from the University of Southern California. She operated a pharmacy with her husband, along with raising children. For Rose and her family, her physical incapacities were as distressing, if not more so, than her memory impairment.

On the day after arriving at Silverado, Rose was able to rise from her bed and take part in a sing-along. Within weeks, she was walking the halls and handling her own spoon, fork, and knife in the dining room. Then she won the baseball-throw competition at the local Senior Olympics.

"My mother participates in activities from eight in the morning until eight at night," declared joyfully her daughter Dr. Janie Williams, who holds a doctorate in nutrition. "She sings, she cooks, she participates in travel club, she goes on outings. Once or twice, I have asked her if she would like to take a nap during the day and she never wants to. She is living her life, loving her life."

Anyone who has experienced the anguish of a loved one's progressive memory-impairment can understand how Rose's vibrancy has brought joy to her family.

"Silverado enables us to enjoy being together and to do things together, and it's wonderful," Dr. Williams said.

———————

Rodney was a man of the cloth. For decades, he tenderly ministered to those in his flock during their most important moments. His grace and compassion made a wedding's joy even brighter, the sorrow of a memorial service more bearable.

You would never have guessed this about Rodney had you seen him the day he was rolled into Silverado on a gurney. He wore a hospital gown deeply stained with food. A sticky dark substance smeared his face. The Silverado caregivers who gathered around him as he entered the front door feared it was blood. Then they realized it was chocolate pudding, never cleansed from his mouth and cheeks after an attempt to feed him.

Staff at the nursing home where he'd been living had tied down his hands and feet. "He lashes out physically and he yells all the time," they said. They couldn't, and didn't want to, care for him anymore.

Tamara, one of the Silverado staff greeting Rodney, took his hand and leaned down toward his ear. "Welcome," she said. "We love you. You are safe here. We are so glad you have come to live with us."

She and the other caregivers took Rodney to his room. When they lifted him from the gurney, they found he was lying on a plastic cup containing several pills. The medicine had clearly been meant for Rodney to take. No one at the nursing home noticed they were tying him down on top of it. The cup's rim had pushed a deep circular groove in his back. The bright red indentation must have been painful.

The caregivers rubbed a healing balm on Rodney's back. They cleaned him, dressed him in fresh and respectable clothes, and arranged his few things within his sight on his dresser. All the while, they continued to tell him he was loved, that he had come to a safe place.

Rodney was near the end of his time on earth. He no longer possessed the ability to speak. But those around him at Silverado remember Rodney as an exceptionally peaceful man. He never raised a hand, never kicked, and never cried out. His expression was often contemplative, radiating a spirituality that made words unnecessary.

Silverado's caregivers didn't fear Rodney, no matter what others had said about him. And so they gave Rodney what he had given so many others during his life. A warm welcome. Compassion. Safety.

Love.

Chapter Nine
Compassionate Caregiving

*I believe that every single event in life happens in
an opportunity to choose love over fear.*

Oprah Winfrey

For more than a decade, Andrea cultivated customers and closed deals in the automotive industry. Eager to hone more business skills, she moved on to become a loan officer and a real estate agent. With the recession weighing heavily on those sectors, she began plotting her next career move and landed an interview for a managerial position at a conference center.

On the way home from that meeting, a sign caught her eye: Silverado Senior Living, care for people with Alzheimer's disease and other memory impairments.

"I wonder if they have any openings," she thought.

The silent question startled the woman who had always carved her achievements in numbers and transactions. She braked, turned into the driveway, and parked.

Andrea hadn't set foot in a senior care community since her childhood, when she was taken to visit elderly relatives in a nursing home. She had no experience, professional or personal, with memory impairment. In fact, she didn't have any idea what to expect as she pulled open the front door to Silverado.

She discovered sparkling lights, greenery and music filling the foyer. People were grouped on plush couches and easy chairs, some chatting, others absorbed in the melodies heralding the approaching holidays.

"It took my breath away," Andrea recalled later. "It was so beautiful and I could feel so much warmth."

Andrea crossed to the reception desk, introduced herself and asked if there were any openings for staff. "You are welcome to take a seat and someone will be right out to speak with you," she was told. Andrea sat on a divan near the Christmas tree, next to a white-haired man. He turned and smiled at her.

"What's your name?" he asked.

"Andrea," she said. "What's yours?"

"George," he replied. Then he smiled again. "You are a beautiful woman." George spoke the compliment from the heart. His sincerity and sweetness moved Andrea deeply.

In that instant, a few minutes after walking into Silverado for the first time, Andrea couldn't have put a name to what had just happened. But it meant something, she was certain.

She quickly learned there were no openings that fit her experience, but Silverado was looking for a caregiver. Andrea found herself saying, "I would like to apply." She was hired, which might seem surprising since she had never worked in health care. But it was clear to those at Silverado that she possessed what's most important: compassion.

The first few weeks were nerve-wracking. Andrea constantly

wondered what she had gotten into. Being a caregiver was demanding in a way that her most hectic days in business had never been. The first time she was called upon to help a male resident in the bathroom was a shock.

"But I realized I needed to stop thinking about how the task was affecting me. I needed to focus on how important it was to make the resident feel dignified and comfortable in what must have been a very difficult situation for him."

Soon, Andrea began telling her family and friends how much she enjoyed the work. She came home exhausted, but elated in a new way by having conjured a smile, a laugh, a conversation out of a resident. Those around her, she was certain, must have tired of hearing her enthusiastic daily descriptions of Silverado.

Within a short time, Andrea knew that her career was heading in the right direction. With Silverado's support, she obtained certification for an administrator's license in the state of California. The idea of managing a memory-care community's daily operations naturally appealed to the businesswoman in her. But as each day passed, it became clearer to her that she wanted to further her new career in a different way. After being appointed as the community's receptionist, she now says she wants to "learn as much as I can and find a way I can work with residents and families, and also raise awareness of the general public about Alzheimer's."

When Andrea initially walked into Silverado, she was drawn in by the environment of love. It guided her past any anxieties she may have had stepping out of an accustomed career path to venture into an unknown job. Several years after the conversation with George, she knows now that in that moment, she connected with the spirit of a memory-impaired person for the first time and it changed her life.

Love is Greater than Fear.

Loren and Steve believe if other organizations operated on Silverado's love-based principle, significant strides would be made toward solving the shortage of caregivers predicted for the surge of aging baby boomers.

"There are so many people who have an innate desire to care for the frail elderly, but they can't find a place where they can truly do that," said Steve. "For our staff, being at Silverado allows them to express the compassion they could never show in their previous work."

Employees who come to Silverado from other senior care organizations often say that here, they're free to provide the kind of care they've always wanted to offer, but never could: care that's entirely about residents and their families.

Silverado spends a great amount of time looking for people with high levels of compassion. Applicants are tested and interviewed for the attribute. As a result, like Andrea, many employees come to Silverado with a background unrelated to the health field. While they lack experience in caregiving, they have the exceptional empathy Silverado seeks.

The rest then falls into place. Silverado trains all new hires on its own techniques. Topics such as Alzheimer's disease, dementia, infection control, and much more are part of the curriculum. So are Silverado's core philosophies and practices, including the principle of *Love is Greater than Fear*. New staff members are paired with mentors who work side-by-side with them until they are ready to handle their duties on their own. And employees never stop learning at Silverado. Acquiring new knowledge and career advancement are primary values and so the staff is encouraged to participate in a wide range of training programs. The company's affiliated non-profit foundation also offers tuition assistance to employees seeking to make careers in long-term care.

Silverado's extensive training not only benefits staff, it is central to how it has maintained the consistent quality of its care as it has grown over the years, said Dr. Joe W. Ramsdell.

"This comprehensive and ongoing education of all employees means each person understands and supports Silverado's care vision through his or her daily interactions with residents," he said. "This is vitally important in ensuring everyone in Silverado's care has a consistent experience."

Silverado's *Love is Greater than Fear* principle frees staff to devote themselves to residents because they know they will never be criticized for doing what is best for those in their care.

Act from your heart. Provide the kind of care you yearn to give. Do it always. These tenets provide for the consistent special quality of the organization's caregiving, regardless of how large the company becomes.

Silverado's ratio of caregivers to residents is one to seven, significantly lower than the one-to-twelve norm in long-term care. This allows Silverado caregivers to dedicate as much time as is needed to each person in their charge.

An overlap of half an hour allows those on one shift to provide information and recommendations about each resident's condition to oncoming staff. And caregivers at Silverado are just that: their sole duty is hands-on care. They are not what are known as universal workers, who are expected to perform other kinds of duties, too. As a result, the overall staffing far exceeds the industry norm.

The organization fosters an environment of celebration to highlight its love-based resident-centered care vision. Everyone who is part of the Silverado community – residents, staff, and family members – is encouraged to fill out "Caught You Caring" slips that are posted on bulletin boards for all to see. They cite individual employees for their great work with a resident or interaction with other staff.

Employees also write up and circulate Silverado Success Stories throughout the organization, recounting the details of exceptional care. One account tells of a Silverado caregiver who had never traveled on an airplane before and who was asked to escort a memory-impaired client on a flight. When the woman became agitated, the caregiver soothed her with quiet song, impressing fellow passengers and the crew with her compassion.

Another story recounts how a client of Silverado At Home saluted staff for keeping him alive by helping him learn to walk and feed himself again. And yet another describes how a Silverado caregiver calmed the grief of a newly-widowed woman by taking her hand, stepping outside to show her the beauty of moonlight on water as they shared tears and silence.

Silverado retains its staff at a far higher rate than the long-term care industry's notoriously low average. Those studying the nation's caregiver shortage say lack of respect, scant training, and poor opportunities for advancement are major reasons people abandon the field. The corrosive impact of constant employee turnover on the quality of care is well documented. So it's no wonder that Loren and Steve believe that Silverado's love-based approach could improve the lives of those with memory-impairment everywhere.

Love is Greater than Fear provides guidance for employees to interact with one another: Choose your actions and words from the standpoint of love and what's best in certain situations, rather than from fear of potentially negative consequences. And Silverado staff credit the *Love is Greater Than Fear* principle for helping them solve conflict in their families and mend friendships damaged by misunderstandings. Setting aside their worries about rejection and ridicule, they can reach out with kind words that bring fresh richness to relationships.

Angel, a chef at one of Silverado's memory-care communities, recalls that when she was introduced to the *Love is Greater than Fear* principle during an orientation, she thought it sounded far-fetched. Her previous career had been primarily in the restaurant and catering business and it was hard to view a work environment as anything but cut-throat.

It began to make sense to her when she used the principle to address a problem she was having in managing a kitchen employee. Angel's normal style was to tersely announce mandates and hope they would be followed. When that tactic didn't have any effect, the administrator of her Silverado community suggested that she change her approach through *Love is Greater than Fear*. Instead of issuing a command, Angel should address the problem by asking the employee, "What is it that I can do for you that would make completing your tasks easier?" That way, Angel would act from the standpoint of love – that I want to work with you to help you be successful – rather than the fear-based premise of simply giving orders.

The impact was gratifying. It led to a conversation between Angel and the employee about how they might cooperate in the future and everything became better.

As Angel saw the effects of *Love is Greater than Fear* in the workplace, she began to embrace the philosophy in her family life. Ultimately, it dramatically improved her tense relationship with her father.

"I am more open now to thinking about what I can do to help make a situation more positive. Just in this past year, I wrote a letter to my father and used the word love for the first time."

***

For over two decades, Joe worked six days a week at his restaurant and deli. From morning to evening, he welcomed customers, supervised employees, balanced the books, made sure the cuisine was up to standards. Approaching his twenty-third year in the business, he decided to sell the still-thriving enterprise and retire.

While he was driving along on an errand two years later, he noticed a sign for Silverado. Joe had no experience with memory care, either in his career or in his personal life. It wasn't something he'd given much thought. But he found himself pulling into the parking lot, going to the front desk, and asking, "What can I do to help the people at Silverado?"

Joe was hired as an activities assistant and he plunged into the job, launching the community's classical music club. Prior to each gathering, Joe researches and chooses pieces to feature. At the meetings, he makes his presentation, serves sparkling cider for participants to sip as they listen to the music, and then they discuss the day's selections.

The residents' responses to the music touch him deeply. Smiles by a previously somber woman or insightful comments from a normally taciturn gentleman affect him in ways he never considered before.

"When I leave at the end of the day, I'm drained. It is so important to engage each resident every day. That is what I am here for."

Several years after coming to Silverado, he still can't explain exactly why he made that impromptu stop. He realizes he was feeling a void in retirement and wanted to fill it with meaning. But he didn't consciously recognize that at the time.

Loren did not know Joe then, but he understands the reason Joe was drawn to Silverado.

"There are so many accomplished people in a wide variety of fields who find they want to do something with purpose in retirement. If providers gave them an environment of love and creativity, where they can feel the joy of helping others in a powerful way every day, we would see more people choosing to work with the memory-impaired."

Chapter Ten
The Family Experience

*In the sweetness of friendship let there be laughter,
and sharing of pleasures. For in the dew of little
things the heart finds its morning and is refreshed.*

Kahlil Gibran

At Silverado, providing attention and assistance to families of the memory-impaired is as important as serving the people directly in its care. Ever since its founding, the organization has offered support groups for relatives and friends.

"How is everyone feeling?" Werner asked.

There was a long silence. Then Russell spoke up.

"It's lonely."

Werner leaned forward slightly in encouragement and Russell began to speak again.

"I've been in the house by myself for three months and I'm still not used to it. Of course, I'm getting a full night's sleep now that Meredith isn't living there and so from a physical standpoint, I am doing better."

He paused.

"But I feel alone."

Around the table, heads nodded. Philip, Gary, Bert, Vernon and the rest: they understood.

For almost every person on the odyssey of Alzheimer's or other memory-impairing disease, another walks a different path. Their routes parallel for a while. But as the condition progresses, they diverge.

The final destination for the memory impaired is sadly known. What lies over the horizon for those on the other trail – the husbands, wives, companions, adult children – is less obvious. But evident to anyone who has ever taken this unwanted trip is that it is laden with visceral emotions and milestones. Often, especially for spouses and long-time partners, there is also the uncertainty of how to refashion a life no longer defined clearly.

This was why Werner was leading a group discussion among nine men whose spouses were residents of Silverado. During the 12 months that Lucette, Werner's wife of 60 years, resided at Silverado, he visited her 340 days. He made friends with the residents and staff, participated in the family support group and came to view Silverado as an extension of his home. He continued to stop in even after Lucette passed away. Then Veronica, the community's director of resident and family services, asked him if he would be willing to spearhead something new.

"We'd like to add another kind of support group," she said. "It would be for men only and we're hoping you will agree to lead it. There are a number of men whose wives are residing here and they might find it easier to talk about what they're going through if there aren't any ladies present."

Werner thought for a moment. Then he said: "I will be happy to try it if you think it would be worthwhile. But of course you know that I have never run a support group."

Veronica smiled and said: "I'm certain you will know what to do."

On a day soon after, Werner gamely reported to Silverado for his first event in this new role. He had reflected quite a bit since his conversation with Veronica. Werner was a retired international banker. He had decades of experience running meetings, sometimes in more than one language. The skills he honed all those years might be helpful now, he thought.

FAMILY HEALTH

Caregiving is a stressful job in most situations. Studies have shown that husbands caring for ailing wives are at the highest risk of having a stroke. See silveradostory.com/stress

The men had lunch first to relax the atmosphere. Then Werner cleared his throat and asked the question about how everyone was feeling.

The ensuing silence sent a flicker of anxiety through Werner. What if the men found it too hard to discuss personal matters? But after Russell spoke of his loneliness, Vernon jumped in.

"I know what you mean. It's strange realizing that Jessica will never be in the bed beside me again. Often when I wake up, I think at first that she got up for a few minutes to go into the bathroom and that she will be right back," Vernon said. He took a sip of water and continued.

"In the last few months Jessica lived at home, I moved into the guest room. She started thrashing a lot during the night and I wasn't getting any rest. But no bed felt as empty as my bed feels now."

When Vernon finished his comments, everyone remained quiet. Werner prepared to pose another question. But then Bert said:

"I understand what you're saying. I've been by myself for more than a year now, and my children think I am doing fine. I guess in a lot of ways, I am, but missing their mother in bed isn't something I'm going to mention to them." Rueful smiles and a few knowing chuckles greeted Bert's remarks.

In the hour that followed, Werner found that indeed, the men spoke of intimate issues. Perhaps, he thought, it was the first time they had felt at liberty to do so. They came from varying walks of life, but they had in common the male mask of stoicism. They had worn this visage while coping with the changes memory-impairment had wrought upon the women they cherished. Sudden crying jags, anger, hurtful language, the need for help in the bathroom: many of the men had weathered these new behaviors over months, even years, as they cared for their spouses at home. Each had reached the point that his ability to provide care was not sufficient for his wife's needs and so she had moved to Silverado. But they had never spoken to anyone of their pain, which Werner now understood ranged from anguish to depression.

"I have gone through the whole cycle, from the beginning of my wife's symptoms to the end," Werner says now. "I know that one of the hardest things for a spouse is that you don't know where this is going, what to expect." He recalls that when the men got together that first day, they started to make comparisons of their situations. They found comfort, understanding and advice.

As the initial session wrapped up, the men made it clear they wanted the group to continue. Werner leads the males-only luncheon once a quarter. It's been more than a year since his wife's passing and he is in a different phase than the other men, who grapple with their wives' memory-impairment as part of their daily lives. He's a busy man: he consults on international banking, travels, skis, reads – particle physics is a favorite topic – and spends time with his daughter.

"I do feel guilty sometimes, because of all the things I do for myself and enjoy now, without my wife here," he says in a soft voice. "But I understand that life does go on and you have a certain responsibility to live it."

It's clear that Werner gains as much from his participation as its members do.

Ken was shocked the first time the police came to the house and wanted to set up a command post.

He questioned them: "I called to report that my mother is missing. She didn't rob a bank."

At 52, Ken is not leading the life he had imagined for himself when he was younger. He didn't foresee summoning the authorities to search for his mom Marilyn, not just this once, but frequently over a period of years. Nor did he anticipate having to explain to her over and over again for months that she was no longer allowed to drive. Each time Marilyn asked him about it, her anger and sorrow were fresh, as though she just learned the news. Ken never thought that in his middle years, he would leave a career to work in a store one day a week because handling his mother's needs consumed so much of his time.

But of course, Ken didn't expect his mother to develop Alzheimer's disease. The diagnosis came at 70 for Marilyn. Seven years later when the combined efforts of her three sons were no longer sufficient for her care, she moved into Silverado.

Ken has always been close to his mother. Despite a difficult marriage, Marilyn raised her sons with grace, he recalls. The boys always knew they could count on their mom.

"Being a caregiver teaches you how to really love someone," he says. "You embrace what 'honor thy father and mother' truly means. When all of this is over, I will at least be able to say I tried my best."

A decade into his mother's memory impairment, Ken could be considered a care veteran, one who has seen and been through almost everything. But he has been a regular participant at Silverado's monthly support groups ever since Marilyn moved in. He finds talking about his experience helps. "It's an ongoing reinforcement process for what you are doing and feeling," he says. Sharing what he has learned over the years with others brings satisfaction. Perhaps most important is the perspective he gains.

"As a caregiver, you can experience a lot of isolation, even if there are people around you. At times, you feel like you are watching the rest of the world go by and you are in a completely different place because of what you are going through."

But because of the support group, he feels he is not truly alone.

SUPPORT FOR CAREGIVERS

How do I know when it's time to seek help for the care of my loved one in order to maintain my own health?
See silveradostory.com/support

Each week for six months, the women gathered to sew their quilt.

Some had never wielded a needle and thread before. But they were determined to learn, because they were not just making a quilt, but creating a tribute to their husbands. At the same time, the women were stitching together new friendships to sustain them through the loss of their spouses to memory-impairment.

Each of the half a dozen women had joined Silverado's family support group and for the first time met other wives who had long cared for their husbands at home, just as she had done.

"What I was going through with Bruce was something I just didn't talk about with other people," said Bette of caring for her husband of nearly five decades. His condition was diagnosed three years before he came to Silverado. In retrospect, she believes it began to manifest seven or eight years earlier. As it progressed, he became verbally and physically aggressive, a situation she endured, like the others, because of her love and her firm belief in the vow she took for better and for worse.

When she finally acknowledged to herself that she could no longer handle Bruce's care, he moved to Silverado. A simple exchange she had with another support group participant changed her life. Her husband had been aggressive at home, the woman said. Bette drew in her breath in surprise and said, "You, too?" The two looked at each other with understanding. It was the beginning of liberation from the guilt, sorrow, anger and loneliness that each had felt for so long.

Like Bette, the other women found fresh strength through the group. Even their adult children had not comprehended what caring for their memory-impaired fathers had really been like. These new friends understood, didn't criticize their feelings or decisions, and offered unwavering solidarity. It always seemed, said group member Diane, that when one woman was feeling sad, "the rest of us would be in a good place and able to comfort her."

Giving voice to their emotions and gaining perspective lost in the stress of daily caregiving "allowed me to fall in love with my husband all over again," Bette said. "When you are going through this, you can forget how many years of your marriage were wonderful."

The women wanted to get to know each other beyond the experiences they shared as caregivers. Working on a project together would be the ideal way. They decided to make a quilt. Each woman would create a square to honor her husband. For Bruce, it would show a football; he played the sport in his youth. A rose would represent Diane's husband Tom. He had planted a rose garden at every home they had lived in during their 50-year marriage.

Even those who had never sewn before quickly came to relish the weekly stitching sessions in a local sewing shop. There was laughter and the satisfying sense of working alongside others to create something that matters. When the project concluded and the quilt was displayed on the wall at Silverado, the women began considering their next group project. "We don't want to let go of the experience," Diane said.

Chapter Eleven
Lives that Matter

Integrity is the essence of everything successful.

R. Buckminster Fuller

As the nation's new president took the helm, he looked out across the sea of faces and called for a fresh era of responsibility in America. A television screen and three thousand miles separated him from the twelve memory-impaired people seated in a semicircle in the Silverado community in Costa Mesa, California. But he seemed to speak directly to them.

For each one had always had a purpose in life. Some served in wartime. Others assisted the effort on the home front. They raised their kids and held down jobs and home; they volunteered in schools, at churches, for food pantries and hospitals, and in countless other places that matter. When they retired, they looked forward to having more time to contribute to their communities.

Lives don't always turn out according to plan, however, and faltering memories brought the group to Silverado. Here, they helped care for children, tended gardens, worked with animals, painted artwork, built useful things. Each had a meaningful role. But it turned out they wanted more. Following the president's address, they pulled their chairs closer together in the living room and began talking about how they yearned to contribute further. They wanted to volunteer outside of Silverado's doors. They were going to show everyone what the memory-impaired can do.

The Silverado Service Club was born and flourished. Its steering committee meets biweekly to discuss volunteer work in progress and make new plans. Its initial project had residents knitting blankets and delivering them to newborns in a local hospital's maternity wing. Other efforts followed.

Lives with meaning: That was what Loren and Steve and their colleague, the late Jim Smith, envisioned when they established Silverado.

"We will be a purpose-driven organization" was their mantra.

The thousands of memory-impaired people who have begun to walk and feed themselves again at Silverado were given the techniques to accomplish these victories. But Silverado has also provided them the reason.

They walk because they have something to walk toward. They nourish their bodies to participate in life, or as Silverado puts it, LIFE: love, innovation, family and engagement.

And Loren and Steve find themselves in the wondrous position of admiring spectators to the residents who created the Silverado Service Club on their own. They receive assistance from staff at their community, but the vision and desire to contribute to the world as a whole is theirs. Silverado has empowered these residents, taking them farther than even Loren, Steve, or Jim could imagine.

When you rekindle the inner spirit, it can burn brighter and stronger then you ever thought.

Katelyn was 16. She had never met a person with Alzheimer's disease. Neither had her friends. But she was more anxious than any of them, which was odd, because Katelyn was the reason the carload of teens was heading to Silverado that afternoon. Her mother Ellen had recently joined Silverado's San Juan Capistrano, California community as its health care services director. She suggested Katelyn volunteer there. With butterflies in her stomach about the prospect, Katelyn invited several pals to accompany her and was relieved when they agreed.

While her friends were calmer than Katelyn, they wondered what they would encounter. Would the people there look different in some way, say strange things, do something weird?

What the teenagers discovered at Silverado was 180 degrees different from what they had been expecting, Katelyn recalled a year later. "The residents were all normal sweet people who were so nice. The place was so warm and welcoming. When we left that day, we all wanted to come back."

And they did, spending hours participating in activities with residents and helping with events around the community. And then, about two months later, Katelyn's understanding of Silverado deepened further in an unexpected way.

During Katelyn's summer vacation from school, her grandmother Mary Jane experienced a severe health decline. Mary Jane moved into Silverado. Katelyn wanted to be with her grandmother as much as possible. She slept in Mary Jane's room many nights and spent almost every day at the community, leaving only for a couple hours to attend a daily tennis camp. Silverado became Katelyn's community. The residents who had sparked such anxiety in her only a few months before turned out to be some of her closest friends.

"We would walk together and talk and it would take my mind off what was going on with my grandmother. And we would have so much fun, doing things like making cookies or telling stories. There is just something so special about the residents," she concluded.

They were also there to comfort her when Mary Jane passed away. Katelyn will never forget their kindness and she wishes to make a lasting contribution to Silverado. She plans to do it by helping the residents at Silverado's San Juan Capistrano community form their own chapter of the Silverado Service Club. A longtime Girl Scout, Katelyn is setting up the project through the organization's Gold Star Award program, the highest Girl Scout honor. She hopes to involve dozens of other young people in the endeavor and she is passionate about the club's importance.

"I understand now how capable people with Alzheimer's disease are, that they still have so much to give, so much to offer the world. It hurts me to see them not being involved on the outside. We need to do this to change the world's view of people with memory-impairment."

The suggestion by Katelyn's mother that she volunteer at Silverado came with the company's enthusiastic backing. Silverado encourages its staff to bring their kids to work with them as often and for as long as they wish. They can eat as many meals and snacks as they like at no cost to their parents. For employees with small children, this offers an extraordinary solution to the perpetual challenge of child care. Many say the policy helped attract them to the company.

It's the reason that on any given day at Silverado, a newborn slumbers quietly on the lap of a resident who possesses baby-calming secrets known only to those with years of experience. A kindergartner works on counting beyond his fingers under the tutelage of one whose former classroom produced generations of budding scientists and engineers.

Two elementary students and a silver-haired man throw a ball for a Labrador retriever. A junior high-schooler and a resident brush a final coat of varnish onto a table that they built together. A high-school senior planning to major in art helps lead a resident watercolor class.

The generations meet at Silverado. Each teaches and learns, gives and receives, as the generations do everywhere else in the world. This relationship is central to Silverado's living environment. It matters so much that along with welcoming employees' children, Silverado invites schools and after-class programs to its communities on an ongoing basis.

Seventeen-year-old Matt started to volunteer at Silverado when his grandmother moved in two years ago. He has logged 3,000 hours of volunteer work on the premises. Matt spent an entire weekend in his garage at home designing and building a special rolling mailbox that residents can use to distribute letters and packages. His experience has helped him hone his career goals. He would like to become a nurse and join Silverado's staff.

Young people throughout say they have been forever shaped by what they have seen and done at the communities. Jackie is the daughter of an employee at Silverado Sugar Land, Texas. At 17, she has volunteered there for three years. So has her younger sister Michelle. Like Katelyn at Silverado in San Juan Capistrano, Jackie says she was nervous the first time she came to the community, but quickly realized "how alive, how happy a place it is, and then I found that this is what I love to do. This is what I plan to do."

***

Loren was a child when his family moved to the grounds of a psychiatric sanitarium. At first, he was too young to comprehend why the patients were there. To him, they were individuals like anyone else. As he grew older, he began to understand that the world did not recognize them as normal. But Loren's perception never changed.

Each human being has an inner spirit. Even if it is obscured from others, we can connect with it if we try hard enough, he is certain. This is as true for the memory-impaired he now serves as it was for the people with mental illness he knew earlier in life.

Sometimes, when Loren reflects on the journey that led him to establish Silverado, he says he feels God called him to do this work. Nearly 15 years after starting the company, he admits he would never have uttered this unexpected statement when he was scouting investors and wrangling with paperwork in the effort to turn his dream into reality.

"I knew that I felt this way then, but I didn't say it, because I was not sure how it would have been interpreted."

Some closest to Loren feel his beliefs have evolved and deepened over the years because of Silverado. "I have watched my Dad become more spiritual through this process. I think he has a much better understanding of what's important," believes his son Aaron, who was a teenager the year Silverado opened its doors.

Heather, like Aaron, was in her teens when her father Loren took her to Silverado for the first time. He walked with her along the hallways, showing her the memory boxes and explaining why they mattered so much.

Then, spreading his arms wide, he described how residents could stroll through the community and around the grounds without locked doors blocking their way. This encouraged walking and eased restlessness. Some memory-impaired people are thought to have a wandering problem, he said. In fact, they are frustrated at feeling confined, without freedom of movement, without anywhere meaningful to go or anything special to do.

Pausing in the country kitchen, he told her the airy room wasn't only about food. Like the kitchen in any home, it was a place people came together.

When they stepped back into the hall, a man approached them. As he neared, Heather saw his hair was more grey than brown. His body was too thin to carry much muscle. But he held himself with precision and spoke with seriousness.

"Please," he said to Loren. "I can't find my tent and I'm wondering if you know where it is. I need to get back to my company right away."

"Yes, Sergeant Lucas, I do know where it is," Loren said to the man in a tone both somber and sincere, one that reflected the important nature of the question. "I would be happy to take you there."

Loren touched the man's back with his palm and the two went down the hallway. Young Heather realized that she was to wait for her father's return. She glanced around and the nearest memory box caught her eye. It displayed several medals, along with black and white photos of a handsome youth in uniform. He appeared just a few years older than she was at the time.

Heather leaned in to read framed newspaper clippings that

were posted beside the pictures. They described military operations in France in 1943. She looked over at the nameplate on the door by the box.

Sergeant Edward Lucas.

Heather turned and peered in the direction of her father and the other fellow, but she didn't see them. She went to a window and looked out. Her dad was crossing Silverado's back garden, taking the man to the place that mattered most in this moment.

Loren was helping Sergeant Lucas find his tent.

Afterword

Government officials, health care experts and business people representing more than two dozen nations around the globe have signed Silverado's guestbook. Executives from other memory-care organizations regularly tour our communities and offices taking photos and notes. We're often asked why we "give Silverado's secrets away to the competition." But to us, no one who cares about memory-impaired individuals is a rival. He or she is a welcome partner in Silverado's vision to transform the daily lives of people with Alzheimer's disease and similar conditions.

Much has happened since we launched Silverado with one memory-care community in 1996. The organization has expanded to encompass numerous locations in multiple states and we now offer home care, care management and hospice.

Silverado's academic affiliations have grown, too. The University of California, San Diego's partnership with our first community led to relationships with other acclaimed academic institutions. They include the University of California, Los Angeles; University of California, Irvine; University of California, San Francisco; University of Southern California; Stanford University; University of North Texas;

Baylor College of Medicine; and the University of Utah. Through these affiliations, Silverado's residents and staff serve as invaluable resources in the research, teaching and care practices designed to better the lives of the memory-impaired everywhere.

The book "Alive with Alzheimer's," by Cathy Stein Greenblat, released by The University of Chicago Press in 2004, has spread Silverado's message around the globe. Rutgers University Professor Emeritus of Sociology and author Greenblat spent two months at one of our communities, where she photographed and interviewed residents, their families and staff. The book has been distributed widely. Her photos of Silverado have been exhibited across the United States, Europe, Scandinavia, Japan and India. We constantly receive correspondence from individuals and organizations galvanized by Cathy's portrayal of the vibrant daily life at Silverado.

We are honored to be asked to speak on a regular basis at regional, national and international conferences. So, as we had hoped from the beginning, Silverado's practices have been reaching an ever-increasing global community of professionals and laypeople committed to improving the lives of those with memory impairment.

There is much more to do.

Despite enormous effort by researchers, no drugs or medical procedures for preventing or curing memory-impairing diseases have been found yet. It is critical that the research continue and Silverado supports it in every way through funding, volunteering and our great willingness to share knowledge. But we would also like to see more resources dedicated to improving the lives of people who currently have memory-impairment and those who will develop it in the future. We believe *care* should be on an equal footing with *cure* and that is our reason for writing this book. We want in all ways to raise our voices on behalf of the memory-impaired.

Every day we witness the memory-impaired being rejected by those around them. Yes, their behavior may be frightening to those who realize that in living long enough, he or she could become this way, too. This is why so many people with Alzheimer's and other memory-impairing diseases are locked behind doors in their own homes or warehoused in facilities where few outsiders venture.

And it is why in many senior living communities, residents whose memories are ebbing cease coming to the dining room because no one will sit with them. They don't sign up for activities because they are shunned by contemporaries who don't want to be reminded that they too may be vulnerable. These factors cause the memory-impaired to become isolated, which worsens their symptoms and affects their emotional and physical health.

The condition is not contagious. But those who have it are avoided like the lepers of old, who were shut away until the invention of medications that solved the problem. It's not much different in the twenty-first century for those with memory-impairment. While it is natural to fear illnesses that could lie ahead in one's future, it is cruel to allow this fright to shape how the memory-impaired are treated.

Rather than menace us, the memory-impaired offer the opportunity to act from the best part of our selves. Reach out to them. Visit them in a senior community or adult day center on a regular basis. Talk or spend quiet moments together. Just being present for even a few hours a month will have an impact more powerful than you are likely to imagine.

If you have time to volunteer, participate alongside them in activities. Talk to people in your church or non-profit organizations about getting involved. If you lead a youth group, have the youngsters take part. The effort you give will be rewarded back a thousand-fold by the positive impact.

We encourage you to take steps to care for your own memory. We are elated that the role of mental stimulation, physical exercise, socialization and sound nutrition – key to Silverado since the start – is now widely recognized as a deterrent in slowing memory-impairment.

If there is a history of memory-impairment in your family, take advantage of the memory screening procedures available for detecting the condition in its earliest stages. You may feel you'd rather not know the results. But by identifying it as early as possible, you and your doctor can work together to develop a care regimen that could include lifestyle changes. Drugs exist that can slow the disease's progression and more are sure to be developed.

We have met many people recently who know through early detection that they are in the initial stage of memory-impairment. This information has enabled them to make important choices about how they will live and receive care in the future. They also participate in the larger discussion of how society will care for the growing numbers of memory-impaired.

Our intention is to expand Silverado across the nation. We want to widen Silverado's reach so we can have a positive impact on more individuals and a broader effect on society as a whole.

When our residents go to an art museum, dine in a restaurant, or help run an errand to a store, they prove their rightful place in the world to all who see them.

In meeting with physicians, social workers and other health professionals in the cities and towns we serve to make the case for Silverado's life-affirming approach to care, our staff helps to better the healthcare services available there.

By inviting the public and families to educational and social events at Silverado, we seek to further contribute to the understanding and practices that matter for the memory-impaired. We encourage all who would like to learn about this issue or wish to enjoy the pleasure of new friendships to spend time with us.

We ask that you help in bringing about this transformation:
Embrace this cause with love.
Put aside fear.
Discover that in giving of yourself, you are changed forever.

Loren Shook & Stephen Winner

Scenes from Silverado

We should consider every day lost on which we have not danced at least once. And we should call every truth false which was not accompanied by at least one laugh.

--Friedrich Nietzsche

Nothing describes Silverado as well as experiencing it. Come inside and take a look.

In the Gazebo

Whether Walter was in Silverado's country kitchen, the garden, his room, or elsewhere in the community, Lisa somehow always knew where to find him when she arrived after school. This was no mean feat in a building of 38,000 square feet on a five-acre campus. But it was the kind of bond they had. Lisa, the seven-year-old daughter of a Silverado laundry employee, had been blind since birth. But she knew where Walter was because it was the place she would have chosen to be, too.

That afternoon, Lisa found Walter sitting in the gazebo. Walter spotted her crossing the lawn and broke into a wide grin. "Lisa, I'm over here," he called out. He knew that Lisa's instinct would bring her to him, anyway, but there was just so much pleasure in saying her name.

Lisa's face lit up and she hastened to hug him. They sat and talked for a bit. Then Walter asked the question that Lisa was expecting, the one she hoped he would ask.

"Lisa, can you count to 200 for me?"

"One, two, three," Lisa began. Walter leaned a little closer to her to listen attentively as she continued. He was committed to improving her math skills. Lisa, excellent at the subject, in truth needed no practice. But every time she reached 200 without an error, Walter would congratulate her and the pride in his voice always made her happy.

After she finished counting, Lisa asked Walter, "Am I beautiful?"

"You are the most beautiful little girl there ever was," Walter told her. "Your hair has a soft sheen that reflects the sun. Your complexion would be the envy of little girls everywhere. Believe me, you are a gift from God."

Lisa smiled and bowed her head. She felt for Walter's hand and grasped it. They were both quiet for a while.

Then, Lisa said: "I can count to 400, too."

"I would like to hear that," Walter replied.

Walter was 99. His advancing memory impairment had reduced the size of his brain by one-third, according to scientists, who say the actions of a person in his condition are not guided by intention or comprehension.

But Walter knew exactly what to do for Lisa. She was his purpose.

The Nurse

"How are you today? How are you feeling?"

Silverado's residents were accustomed to hearing this question from Betty every morning. If they said they felt any way other than great, Betty would furrow her brow and ask for details. She cared about their health; they knew that.

Betty was a four-foot eleven-inch dynamo who carried a clipboard so she could make notes on what the residents told her. Meeting her, you would assume she was a member of Silverado's care team. In fact, she was a retired nurse who resided at the community. Her memory impairment meant she could no longer live by herself, but it had not dampened her interest in others. Nor had it erased the instincts she had accumulated over decades. Silverado's staff provided her with the clipboard and welcomed what she had to say.

It was a blow to everyone at Silverado the day a seizure extinguished Betty's vitality and sent her to the hospital. Doctors placed her on a ventilator and told her family that Betty had little time left to live. Betty could not communicate much, but she was able to let her relatives know that she wanted to return to Silverado. It was her home.

Betty was taken back to Silverado and gently tucked in her bed. Silverado Hospice joined the community's team in caring for her. Along with Betty's family, Silverado staff and residents visited her constantly as she lay prone, her eyes closed. They held her hand, talked to her even though they weren't sure she understood, told her they loved her. Caregivers styled her hair each morning and painted her nails. It didn't matter that her life was coming to its conclusion. "We want her to look her best."

Three days after Betty returned from the hospital, Silverado's administrator Carole walked into her room. She was startled to find Betty sitting up, grinning and gazing out the window, where early evening shadows were lengthening into darkness.

"Is it night already?" she asked.

"Yes, it is," said Carole. "The days certainly fly by when we're having so much fun."

Betty chuckled and blew her a kiss. A few days later, she left her bed to take part in a chair exercise program. Then she joined the community's walking group on its daily rounds, only occasionally using a walker for support.

A short time afterwards, Betty was looking out one of Silverado's windows when she saw a staff member take a tumble in the garden. She came outside, clipboard in hand, as several other people were assisting the woman to her feet.

"How are you?" Betty asked, her face creased with concern. "Can I do anything to help? I'm a nurse."

Thank you, they told her. We feel so much better because you are here.

They were all smiling at Betty as they said that, but you didn't have to look closely to see their tears.

Love

Josephine was standing at the entrance again.

She had moved into Silverado the previous week. Since then, she had spent nearly every waking minute in the community's foyer, rattling the handle of the front door and saying, "I want to leave. Please open this door. I want to leave."

The entrance was locked from the inside so staff would know if residents were leaving the premises. All other doors to the exterior opened with a simple push of the hand. They led onto Silverado's secure grounds and people at the community were encouraged to go in and out as much as they liked.

But Josephine didn't want to do anything except jiggle that doorknob. Regardless of how many activities she was asked to join, how many potential new friends she was introduced to, she always darted back to the foyer as soon as she could.

The caregivers were distressed. They wanted Josephine to be happy in her new home. Despite all of Silverado's years of experience in caring for the memory-impaired, no one could figure out how to help her.

On a conference call, caregivers consulted with staff at other Silverado communities. They described how Josephine rattled the door handle for hours every day and how they tried to no avail to involve her in life at Silverado. When they finished talking, there was a moment of silence and then a sudden question from one of those listening.

"Have you told her that you love her?"

The caregivers gasped. No, they hadn't. Everyone had been so worried about Josephine that they hadn't done this simple thing which is so important at Silverado.

From that day on, each time the staff saw Josephine, they hugged her and said, "Josephine, we love you. You are safe here."

Within three weeks, the noise of Josephine rattling the doorknob ceased. It was replaced by the sound of her laughing during the community's club activities, singing in music groups and talking with new friends.

She realized now that she was safe and loved, and that had vanquished her fears.

The Inspection

Since the diagnosis of Wendell's memory impairment four years previously, Joanie had been caring for him at home. She was just a little younger than her 84-year-old husband and he now needed more assistance than she could handle. And so on this morning, Wendell was moving into Silverado. Joanie felt the anguish and loss that come with separating from a beloved spouse, even when there's no doubt it's for the best.

In addition to the sadness of parting, she told Silverado's staff, she was distressed because Wendell had refused to bathe for several weeks. It pained her that this man who had been so meticulous and dashing in his Coast Guard uniform when they first met at a coffee social six decades earlier was arriving at his new home unkempt. Silverado's staff tried to comfort her: This problem is not unusual. We'll make it right. The next time you see him, he will be handsomer than ever.

They helped her arrange pictures of Wendell from his days in the service in his memory box. Then, Joanie told Wendell she would see him the following day and she went outside to her car.

Inside, caregivers talked gently with Wendell about bathing. He refused. They discussed it with him delicately several more times during the afternoon and he continued to say no. As staff shared information about the community's newest resident, employees from all departments learned of this challenge. At Silverado, everyone is considered part of the care team, regardless of his or her official title.

An hour before dinner, Jack, director of maintenance for the community, paused to study Wendell's memory box. The door to Wendell's room was open. Jack tapped on the doorframe and asked if he could come in. Wendell agreed. Jack entered and announced, "Inspection is in 20 minutes. You need to shower and shave right now so you're ready."

Wendell rose to his feet. Jack stepped back into the hall and gestured for assistance from the caregivers, who immediately came to assist Wendell.

When Joanie arrived at Silverado the following day, Wendell was waiting for her in the foyer. His hair was neatly combed, his face freshly shaved, and he emanated the pleasing scent of cologne. She reached out to hold him tight. To Joanie, Wendell didn't look any older than he had when they met at that social. If anything, he seemed to her even more handsome.

The Dance

Dessert plates were cleared away and people sipped their last coffee. Residents left Silverado's dining room for a variety of post-meal pursuits. A group headed to the living room, where they gathered with caregivers in an informal circle.

It had been another busy day, with many get-togethers of all kinds. Now, dusk was softening the sky outside the picture windows. The room was quiet, but not for long.

Janis, a caregiver, inserted ragtime tunes into the CD player and pranced her way to the center of the circle. She smiled toward Mario, the caregiver coordinator. And Mario, who has never considered himself a dancer, found himself shimmying toward her.

Janis took the hand of a graying gentleman, who stood and moved in rhythm. Soon, other pairs of staff and residents were dancing, with some caregivers stooping to partner with those in wheelchairs. When the CD finished, Mario loaded another one into the player, then another.

Had you later asked the residents for details about the evening, they probably couldn't have answered. Memory impairment ravages short-term recollection. But remembering the event isn't important. What matters is experiencing the joy.

"When I'm at Silverado, I don't want to leave," Mario said a few days later in response to a question about his work. "And when I'm not at Silverado, I think about it, about what's happening here."

He fell silent. He couldn't find words to explain exactly why he feels this way. He didn't need to.

Have a Cup of Coffee

Max visited Jeanne every day during the seven years that his wife resided at Silverado.

Weekdays, weekends, holidays, good and bad weather: nothing changed Max's routine of rising from his bed in their long-time home just after dawn and driving two and a half miles to the community to be with Jeanne.

Their relationship had always been like this. "From the moment I met her, I worshipped her," said Max.

Fifty-seven years after that New Year's Eve when he picked Jeanne up at her house on a blind date, his voice catches when he describes how "the door opened and there stood an angel."

So when Jeanne's memory impairment led to a breakdown

and it was clear she needed more assistance than Max could give, Silverado became as much a part of his life as his wife's. It was where he got his morning cup of coffee and read the newspaper, where he spent most of the day.

And it was where he made new friendships, including with Angel, the chef. They forged their bond as they worked together to create foods that would tempt Jeanne and that she would be able to eat as her ability to chew and swallow ebbed.

Then his wife passed away. He moved numbly through the busy days that followed: visits by family and friends, arrangements of all kinds, the memorial service.

The morning after the last relative left town, Max rose at his customary time, got in the car, and headed toward Silverado. He was halfway to the community when he remembered his wife no longer lived there.

He kept on driving.

Smiles and hugs welcomed him when he arrived at Silverado. Just like every other day for the past seven years, Max poured a cup of coffee and took a look at the newspaper. Then he walked through the community to make sure he said hello to all of the residents and staff.

And he has returned to Silverado ever since, repeating this morning routine before heading out to tutor a third-grade boy at a nearby school and to other volunteer work.

When family and friends ask Max why he keeps going to Silverado, he chuckles and replies, "They have the best coffee in town."

Then he adds:

"Come with me and try a cup."

ACKNOWLEDGMENTS

There are so many people who have helped Steve and me to bring this book to reality and who have made Silverado what it is today. I first met Vance Caesar in 1995 when I was putting together the seeds of the concept of Silverado. Vance was my professional coach, guiding and challenging me through the various steps of forming a company. Thankfully, he is still my coach and mentor today and serves on the Board of Silverado Senior Living.

I would like to acknowledge Chris Lewis and Pat Haden, partners in the equity firm, Riordan Lewis Haden. They didn't invest in start-up companies but agreed to meet with Silverado co-founder Jim Smith and me to offer guidance about venture capital partners. A few months after our initial meeting, not only did they invest their money in our idea, but Chris joined our Board of Directors and has been an invaluable source of guidance and a catalyst for innovation since 1997. Chris, Pat and the more recent partners of RLH are valued colleagues. It has been Silverado's honor to serve Pat's mother, Helen, and his family and Chris's mother, Penny, and his family too.

Steve and I have the privilege of working with an excellent team of senior executives. Senior Vice President of Operations Jack Peters has been a friend and business colleague of mine for over 25 years. We are also proud to work with Chief Financial Officer Tom Croal, Chief Administrative Officer Dawn Usher, Senior Vice President of Sales and Marketing Mark Mostow, Senior Vice President of Clinical Services Anne Ellett, Senior Vice President of Silverado Hospice and Silverado At Home Randy Platt, and Regional Vice Presidents of Operations Kathy Greene and Michelle Egerer.

Moving beyond the executive team, we want to acknowledge

other vice presidents, senior directors, regional directors and directors in our corporate group: Rick Barker, Rita Chiao, Debi Salisbury, Beth Burbage, Mark Nease, Frank Russo, Paul Mullin, Stan Tanabe, Pam Huffman, Nicholas Giampietro, Deborah Swanner, DeAnna Lyons, Sarah McSpadden, Lori Muehlbauer, Joanne Fetgatter, Sue Kruse, Denise Graham, Beth McCurdy, Sue Arnheiter, Steve Taylor, Nancy Convertito, Paula Little, Carilyn Long, Kathy Mahan and Robyn Philips. And for me, nothing is possible without my trusted and ever-energetic assistant, Dorine Sterner, who keeps me organized and maximizes my efficiency.

Our administrators lead and manage the complexities of service including staffs that often exceed 100 people serving our residents, clients and patients. These leaders are the ones who embody our core operating philosophy, *Love is Greater than Fear*. Steve and I want to express our deep gratitude to Senior Administrators Daizel Gasperian, Vida Gwinn, Le Riggs and Noralyn Snow and to Administrators Jolene Farish, Carole Shaw, Sharon Lutz, Monica Westphaln, Rachelle Dardeau, Jean Busher, Liana Constantinescu, Maria Quizon, Laura Avanesyan, Tracey Truscott, Annelle Travis, Kelli Clarke, Kathleen DeLeo, Chris Holland, Leslie Church, Elizabeth Montana, Dawn Kuser, Rachael Kleczkowski, Patricia Blunt, Cindy S. Scott, Kathryn Mize, Court Riddle, Kimberly Dansie and Amber McCord.

Our many Medical Directors constantly strive to work with our leaders, staff and geriatric professionals to ensure we deliver world class care. Our thanks to Dr. Joseph Ramsdell, Dr. Jeffry Cummings, Dr. Elizabeth Landsverk, Dr. Torsten Kruse, Dr. Alan Weinberger, Dr. David Trader, Dr. Daniel Osterweil, Dr. John Daly, Dr. Patricia Gifford, Dr. Habib Bashoura, Dr. Berry McCord, Dr. John Duffy, Dr. Simin Torabzadeh, Dr. Stephen Fehlauer, Dr. James Wood, Dr.

Fares Arguello, Dr. Janet Nguyen, Dr. Gary Salzman, Dr. Suleman Lalani, Dr. Ursula Braun, Dr. Joyce Thompson, Dr. Michael Chang, Dr. Kojo Pobee, Dr. George Danial, Dr. Loren Novak and Dr. Joseph Roosth. We greatly appreciate the thousands of physicians, nurse practitioners, nurses, social workers and geriatric care professionals who work tirelessly each day throughout our country in order to make life better for our seniors.

Many people - families, staff and other professionals - over the years have suggested we write a book. Author Shannon Ingram, Silverado's senior director of marketing communications and Audrey Knoth of Goldman & Associates Public Relations, helped Steve and me to turn those suggestions into reality. Their unique passion, coupled with know-how and incessant prodding kept us on track. Shannon and Audrey were assisted by the capable team of Patty Ledezma, Marcelo Soares, Tara Zoumer, Sean Glumace, Marilyn Goldman, Lia Segerblom, Laren Bright and Ellen Reid.

We are grateful to the people who helped us tell our story who are not acknowledged elsewhere: Angel Vierna, Sheila Alston, David Pascoe, Maryam Mahbod, Dr. Janie Williams, Alex Abbiate, Jim Monahan, Jackie Jonovic, Linda Szemenyei, Max White, Joe Russo, Andrea Furch-Coultas, Leslie Bethge, Teri Orr, Linda Silverton, Judy Kunkle, David Baer, Werner Sommer, Linda Lavison, Ken Nelson, Veronica Arellano, Ellen Sloan, Katelyn Sloan, Matt Phillips, Ruth Ann Chase, Jackie Chase, Michelle Chase, Pat Thompson, Diane Nevotti and Bette Schwager.

I appreciate my important mentors through the years, James Conte, Robert Green and my brother and sister-in-law, Larry and Jean Shook. And I give thanks to my pastor, Rick Warren, whose sermons and writings have helped in so many ways he will never know.

We have been blessed by long time friends and colleagues who support the Silverado vision of giving LIFE – David Burroughs, Bruce Glaser and Dave Lahr of Centerpointe Construction, whose expertise and dedication make the often complex renovations and construction a reality. Doug Pancake brings architectural skills to help us create physical plant innovations that empower our residents to experience freedom again.

We are grateful to the leaders, researchers and faculty at the many teaching and research centers that affiliate with Silverado: University of California San Diego, University of Southern California, University of California Irvine, Stanford University, University of California San Francisco, Baylor University, University of Utah and University of North Texas. In particular, we thank Dr. Gerald Davison, Professor of Gerontology and Psychology at the University of Southern California, Dean, Leonard Davis School of Gerontology, Executive Director, Ethel Percy Andrus Gerontology Center, for his pioneering work and extraordinary leadership in education and USC's critical research in the field of Gerontology. And thanks to the Erickson School of Aging at the University of Maryland for their pioneering efforts to expand the number of leaders in our profession. Such excellent schools play an essential role in preparing our nation to serve the tidal wave of seniors coming our way by 2030.

Our partnership with the Alzheimer's Association and its many chapters has been invaluable, as well as all of the non-profit senior service organizations we work with around the country. We thank our many industry partners, especially the leadership and volunteers of the Assisted Living Federation of America, American Seniors Housing Association and the National Investment Center for the Seniors Housing and Care Industry.

Sincere thanks to the many lenders and support staff in the financial markets whose expertise and resources have helped to make our services possible – George Chapman and Mike Stephen at Healthcare REIT, for taking a risk in the beginning to see and support our vision; Red Capital; Fannie Mae; and to Don Ambrose, our trusted mortgage broker from the beginning.

Thanks to the many children of Silverado staff, families and volunteers. You brighten the days of our residents with your energy, companionship and the ways you embody purpose and hope for the future.

My faithful companion and silent partner who has always wanted to be by my side and usually is whenever I'm at Silverado's home office or in our communities and offices in Southern California is Candy Shook, my beloved Labrador Retriever who serves as chief pet officer. Steve's beloved companion is Truffles, a chocolate Schipperke. Candy, Truffles and their hundreds of friends, be they four-footed, feathered or swimming in our fish tanks, are invaluable servants providing comfort, companionship and helping to re-engage people in life who have been dealt a hard blow by a fate none of us want. These pets do this tirelessly and without complaint, always giving and receiving love, even when the recipient of their affection cannot speak.

To the thousands of residents, clients and patients that we have served and are serving along with the tens of thousands of family members who have put their trust in Silverado to care for their loved ones in a time of great need, we send you our most sincere love and gratitude. It is an honor to serve each and every one of you. We consider serving you to be the same as caring for our mothers, fathers or spouses.

And finally, we extend heartfelt thanks to the thousands of Silverado associates and their families, for their commitment and passion to join us in our journey and to change the world in the way the memory-impaired are served, to give LIFE to our clients at home, our residents in communities and to our hospice patients, their families as well as to each other. Individually we can touch a few lives. Together, with *LOVE>fear* as our guide, we can touch the world.

Loren Shook

www.silveradostory.com

SOURCES

Susan Stein Frazier, Project Guide, Green House Project

Cathy Greenblat, Professor Emeritus of Sociology, Rutgers University, Rutgers, New Jersey

Susan Harnett, Reference Librarian, Eastern Virginia Medical School, Norfolk, Virginia

Joe W. Ramsdell, M.D., Professor and Division Head, General Internal Medicine at the University of California, San Diego

Alzheimer's Association

Flynn, Robert J. and Lemay, Raymond A. *A Quarter-Century of Normalization and Social Role Valorization*. Ottawa: University of Ottawa Press, 1999

Fuchs, Elinor. *Making an Exit*. New York: Metropolitan Books, 2005

Shenk, David. *The Forgetting, Alzheimer's: Portrait of an Epidemic*. New York: Doubleday, 2001

Scandinavian Journal of Disability Research, Vol. 8, No. 4. 2006: "Bengt Nirje in Memoriam," by Mårten Söder

Canadian Psychology, February 2001: Review of Flynn and Lemay's *A Quarter-Century of Normalization and Social Role Valorization* by Aldred Neufeldt

The Social Role Valorization Implementation Project

Wikipedia: "Normalization," "Wolf Wolfensberger"

Better Care Better Jobs

Fairfax Hospital, Kirkland, Washington

GLOSSARY

The following terminology is often used by medical professionals in discussing memory-impairing diseases and memory care. Additional glossaries offer further information on Silverado Senior Living's website: www.SilveradoSenior.com.

acetylcholine
A chemical in the brain (neurotransmitter) that appears to be involved in learning and memory. Acetylcholine is greatly diminished in the brains of people with Alzheimer's disease.

activities of daily living (often called ADLs)
Personal care activities necessary for everyday living, such as eating, bathing, grooming, dressing and using the toilet.

adjuvant therapy
Treatment provided in addition to primary treatment.

alleles
One of the different forms of a gene that can exist at a single locus (spot on a chromosome) or site.

Alzheimer's disease
A dementia characterized by progressive mental impairment and by the presence of excessive neurofibrillary tangles and senile plaques.

amyloid
A waxy translucent substance consisting of protein in combination with polysaccharides that is deposited in some animal organs and tissues under abnormal conditions (such as Alzheimer's disease).

amyloid plaque
Build up of amyloid protein and a primary hallmark of Alzheimer's disease.

amyloid precurser protein (often called APP)
A gene, when mutated, that causes an abnormal form of the amyloid protein to be produced.

agnosia

Literally a condition of not knowing: the inability to recognize sensory stimuli. Color agnosia is the inability to recognize colors. Visual agnosia is the inability to recognize objects in the presence of intact visual sensation.

agraphia

An acquired condition of impaired or absent writing ability.

akathisia

A condition of extreme motor restlessness. It is accompanied by subjective feelings of anxiety and restlessness.

akinesia

A state of lowered motor activity.

amygdala

One of the structures of the limbic system set of brain structures, important in memory and in the regulation of emotion.

anomia

Sometimes known as "dysnomia," it is a condition in which the patient has difficulty finding correct words.

aphasia

An acquired inability to use certain aspects of language. It can be either an expressive or a receptive language disorder. "Aphasia" is a very broad term that is made more useful by descriptive qualifiers indicating the type of language impairment involved.

apraxia

Impaired ability to perform previously chained skills in a continuous behavior. Construction apraxia is an impairment in reproducing patterns; it is assessed by observing drawing and drafting or by having the patient build three-dimensional objects. Ideational apraxia refers to impairment in the idea of the required behavior; it is usually assessed by asking the patient to perform several linked behaviors. Ideomotor apraxia refers to the inability to demonstrate motor behaviors that were known in the past; it is assessed by asking the patient to pantomime a task, such as using a can opener or a pair of scissors.

ataxia
Loss or failure of muscular coordination. Movement, especially gait, is clumsy and appears to be uncertain. Ataxic patients often sway while walking. Ataxia usually results from an inaccurate sense of position in the lower limbs. Difficulty with gait increases greatly when the patient is asked to walk with eyes closed.

atonia
Complete lack of muscle tone.

atrophy
Shrinkage of (brain) tissue due to loss of neuronal processes.

auditory verbal dysnomia
An aphasic deficit characterized by impairment of ability to understand the symbolic significance of verbal communication through the auditory avenue (loss of auditory-verbal comprehension).

autonomic nervous system
That part of the nervous system concerned with visceral and involuntary functions.

beta amyloid
An amyloid derived from a larger precursor protein; it is a component of the neurofibrillary tangles and plaques characteristic of Alzheimer's disease.

beta-secretase
An enzyme that catalyses the splitting of interior peptide bonds in a protein. Beta-secretase acts by trimming off a protein protruding from a brain cell. This small snip is thought to be the first step in the buildup of microscopic balls of debris known as amyloid that are toxic to brain cells.

bradykinesis
A motor disorder, frequently seen in Parkinson's disease, which results from rigidity of muscles and which is manifested by slow finger movements and loss of fine motor skills such as writing.

celecoxib
An anti-inflammatory drug thought to reduce Alzheimer's risk in persons with a family history of dementia.

cerebrovascular disease
Disease of the cerebrum and the blood vessels supplying it.

cerebrospinal
Of or relating to the brain and spinal cord or to these together with the cranial and spinal nerves that innervate voluntary muscles.

cholinesterase inhibitors
Class of drugs known to delay the breakdown of acetylcholine.

corpus callosum
The brain structure that connects the right and left hemispheres.

declarative memory
Recalling newly-learned information about people, places and things.

delirium
An acute global impairment of cognitive functioning. Delirium is usually reversible and is mostly due to metabolic disturbances of brain function.

dementia
A condition, usually chronic, of global impairment of cognition that occurs in the absence of clouded consciousness. In many cases, such as in Alzheimer's disease, the condition is progressive.

donepezil
A drug currently approved in preventing the development of Alzheimer's in people diagnosed with mild cognitive impairment.

dopamine
A drug currently approved in preventing the development of Alzheimer's in people diagnosed with mild cognitive impairment.

dysarthria
Acquired impairment in motor aspects of speech. Dysarthric speech may sound slurred or compressed. Spastic dysarthria, associated with pseudo-bular palsy, is low in pitch and has a raspy sound, with poor articulation. Flaccid dsyarthria, associated with bulbar palsy, has an extremely nasal aspect to its sound. Ataxic dysarthria is associated with cerebellar palsy and produces deficits in articulation and prosody. Hypokinetic dysarthria, found with parkinsonism, results in low-volume speech and less emphasis on accented syllables; there are also articulatory initiation difficulties. Hyperkinetic dysarthria results in prosodic, phonation, and articulatory deficits; the loudness and accents of speech are uncontrolled. Many disorders present with combinations of the different types of dysarthria.

dysfluency
A disturbance of the fluency of speech.

dysphagia
Difficulty in swallowing.

dystonia
Involuntary, slow movements that tend to contort a part of the body for a period of time. Dystonic movements tend to involve large portions of the body and have a sinuous quality that, when severe, resembles writhing.

fronto-temporal dementia
This term covers a range of conditions, including Pick's disease, frontal-lobe degeneration and dementia associated with motor neuron disease. All are caused by damage to the frontal lobe and/or the temporal parts of the brain, the areas responsible for behavior, emotional responses and language skills.

gamma secretase
An enzyme partly responsible for plaque buildup in the brain characteristic of Alzheimer's.

geriatric psychiatrist
A specialist in the branch of medicine concerned with both the prevention of illness in older people and with psychiatry.

hippocampus
An area buried deep in the forebrain that helps regulate emotion and memory.

hydrocephalus
Abnormal accumulation of cerebrospinal fluid within the cranium, producing enlarged ventricles and compression of neural tissue.

Korsakoff's syndrome
Deterioration of the brain and cognitive abilities (particularly memory) caused by chronic and severe alcohol abuse and resulting thiamine deficiency.

Lewy Body dementia
Lewy Body dementia is characterized by distinct cognitive impairment with fluctuating confusion, disturbance of consciousness, visual hallucinations, delusions, falls, and significant parkinsonism. The hallmark feature is the widespread Lewy bodies throughout the neo and archi cortex with the presence of Lewy body and cell loss in the subcortical nuclei.

mild cognitive impairment (often called MCI)
A syndrome of memory impairment that does not significantly affect daily activities and is not accompanied by declines in overall cognitive function.

micrographia
Writing with very minute letters or only on a small portion of a page. Sometimes seen in patients with seizure disorders.

neurodegenerative
Relating to or characterized by degeneration of nervous tissue.

neurofibrillary tangles
A fine fiber found in cytoplasm signaling an abnormality of the hippocampus and neurons of the cerebral cortex that occurs especially in Alzheimer's disease.

neuroleptics
A term that refers to the effects of antipsychotic drugs on a patient, especially on his or her cognition and behavior.

neuropsychiatrist
A specialist in the medicine concerned with both neurology and psychiatry.

neuropsychological
Concerned with the integration of psychological observations on behavior and the mind with neurological observations on the brain and nervous system.

neuropsychologist
A psychologist who has completed special training in the neurobiological causes of brain disorders, and who specializes in diagnosing and treating these illnesses using a predominantly medical (as opposed to psychoanalytical) approach.

non-pharmacological
Various strategies aimed at managing problematic behaviors, including therapy, changes in the home or environment and the use of appropriate communication techniques.

nystagmus
A spasmodic movement of the eyes, either rotary or side-to-side.

paraphasia
A disturbance in the verbal output of a patient. A literal paraphasia involves the substitution of letters in a word, for example, "ridilicous" for "ridiculous." Semantic or verbal paraphrasia involves the substitution of one word for another. The two words are usually in the same semantic class: for example, "shirt" for "pants."

paranoid delusion
An abnormal mental state characterized by suspiciousness and/or persecutory trends.

parathesia
Abnormalities of sensation, especially tactile and somesthetic sensation.

Parkinson's disease
A disorder that primarily affects the motor functions of the cerebellum. Parkinson's disease is characterized by tremors and gait disturbances.

PET
Stands for positron emission tomography, which is a highly specialized imaging technique using short-lived radioactive substances. This technique produces three-dimensional colored images.

Pick's disease
A form of dementia that affects the frontal and temporal lobes and that is characterized by early loss of social grace and inhibition.

plaque
A localized abnormal patch on a body part or surface.

presenile dementia
Severe deterioration of mental functions before the age of 65. Most contemporary investigators minimize the utility of the distinction between presenile and senile dementias.

pseudodementia
Any form of apparent cognitive impairment that is not global and that mimics dementia. A common form is pseudodementia secondary to depression.

senile dementia
Severe deterioration of mental functions in persons over the age of 65 years. See presenile dementia.

senile plaques
Areas of incomplete necrosis found in persons with primary neuronal degenerative diseases of the brain. Senile plaques can also be found, in the absence of overt pathology, in most elderly people.

strabismus
Lack of muscle coordination such that both eyes cannot be directed to the same object.

synapse
The space between the terminal end of an axon and another cell body. Neurotransmitters are released in the synapse and carry signals from one nerve cell to another.

transient ischemic attacks (often called TIA's)
Brief episodes of insufficient blood supply to selected portions of the brain.

ventricles
The spaces within the brain through which cerebrospinal fluid circulates.

Wernicke's aphasia
An acquired inability to communicate verbally due to impairment of receptive abilities. Associated with lesions in the posterior portion of the dominant hemisphere.

RESEARCH AFFILIATIONS (PAST & PRESENT)

Silverado Senior Living
6400 Oak Canyon, Suite 200
Irvine, CA 92618
Phone: 949-240-7200 or 888-328-5400
Web Site: http://www.silveradosenior.com

Administration on Aging
One Massachusetts Avenue NW
Washington, DC 20001
Phone: 202-619-0724
Website: http://www.aoa.gov/AoARoot/Index.aspx

Alzheimer's Association
225 N. Michigan Ave., Fl. 17
Chicago, IL 60601
24/7 Helpline: 1-800-272-3900
Web Site: http://www.alz.org

A Place for Mom
221 - 1st Ave West, Suite 350
Seattle, WA 98119
Phone: 206-285-4666
Phone for Care: 1-877-MOM-DAD9 (1-877-666-3239)
Web Site: http://www.aplaceformom.com/

Assisted Living Federation of America
1650 King St., Suite 602
Alexandria, VA 22314
Phone: 703-894-1805
Web Site: http://www.alfa.org/

Leeza's Place
9000 Sheridan St., Suite 115
Pembroke Pines, FL 33024
Phone: 1-888-OK-Leeza (1-888-655-3392)
Web Site: http://www.leezasplace.org

National Association of Professional Geriatric Care Managers
3275 West Ina Road, Suite 130
Tucson, AZ 85741
Phone: 520-881-8008
Web Site: http://www.caremanager.org/

National Family Caregivers Association
10400 Connecticut Avenue, Suite 500
Kensington, MD 20895
Phone: 301-942-6430
Web Site: http://www.nfcacares.org

National Senior Living Providers Network
Phone (NSLPN Career Network): 407-705-3056 ext. 301
Web Site: http://nslpn.com/

Azusa Pacific University
901 E. Alosta Ave., PO Box 7000
Azusa, CA 91702-7000
Phone: 626-969-3434
Web Site: http://www.apu.edu/

Baylor College of Medicine
One Baylor Plaza
Houston, TX 77030
Phone: 713-798-4951
Web Site: http://www.bcm.edu/

California State University Fullerton
800 N. State College Blvd.
Fullerton, CA 92831
Phone: 657-278-2011
Website: http://www.fullerton.edu/

California State University-Long Beach
1250 Bellflower Blvd.
Long Beach, CA 90840
Phone: (562) 985-4111
Web Site: http://www.csulb.edu/

California State University Los Angeles
5151 State University Dr.
Los Angeles, CA 90032
Phone: 323-343-3000
Web Site: http://www.calstatela.edu/

George G. Glenner Alzheimer's Family Center
3702 4th Ave.
San Diego, CA 92103
Phone: 619-543-4700
Web Site: http://www.alzheimerhelp.org/

Golden West College
15744 Goldenwest St.
Huntington Beach, CA 92647
Phone: 714-892-7711
Web Site: http://www.goldenwestcollege.edu/

Grossmont College
8800 Grossmont College Dr.
El Cajon, CA 92020
Phone: 619-644-7000
Web Site: http://www.grossmont.edu/

Kingwood College
5000 Research Forest Dr.
The Woodlands, TX 77381
Phone: 832-813-6500
Web Site: http://www.lonestar.edu/kingwood

Mira Costa College
One Barnard Drive
Oceanside, CA 92056
Phone: 760-757-2121
Web Site: http://www.miracosta.edu/

Palomar College
1140 West Mission Rd.
San Marcos, CA 92069
Phone: 760-744-1150
Web Site: http://www.palomar.edu/

San Diego City College
1313 Park Blvd.
San Diego, CA 92101
Phone: 619-388-3400
Web Site: http://www.sdcity.edu/

San Diego State University (School of Social Work)
5500 Campanile Dr.
San Diego, CA 92182
Phone: 619-594-6865
Web Site: http://chhs.sdsu.edu/sw/

University of California Irvine (School of Medicine)
1001 Health Sciences Rd.
Irvine, CA 92697
Phone: 949-824-5926
Web Site: http://www.som.uci.edu/

University of California-Los Angeles
(Alzheimer's Disease Center)
10911 Weyburn Ave., Ste. 200
Los Angeles, CA 90095
Phone: 310-794-2553
Web Site: http://www.eastonad.ucla.edu/index.asp

University of California San Diego
(Shiley Marcos Alzheimer's Disease Research Center)
8950 Villa La Jolla Dr., Suite C129
La Jolla, CA 92037
Phone: 858-622-5800
Web Site: http://adrc.ucsd.edu/index.html

University of La Verne
1950 Third St.
La Verne, CA 91750
Phone: 909-593-3511
Web Site: http://www.ulv.edu

University of North Texas
1155 Union Cir.
Denton, TX 76203
Phone: 940-565-2000
Web Site: http://www.unt.edu/

University of Utah, Department of Educational Psychology
1705 Campus Center Dr., Room 327
Salt Lake City, UT 84112
Phone: 801-581-7148
Web Site: http://www.ed.utah.edu/EDPS/

USC Davis School of Gerontology
3715 McClintock Ave.
Los Angeles, CA 90089
Phone: 213-740-6060
Web Site: http://www.usc.edu/dept/gero/

Vanguard University
55 Fair Dr.
Costa Mesa, CA 92626
Phone: 714-556-3610
Web Site: http://www.vanguard.edu/

SUGGESTED READING

All of these books can be purchased through Silverado's Online Store at: http://astore.amazon.com/silvsenilivi-20

Avadian, Brenda. *"Where's My Shoes?": My Father's Walk Through Alzheimer's*. North Star Books, 2005

Bell, Virgina. *A Dignified Life: The Best Friends Approach to Alzheimer's Care, A guide for Family Caregivers*. Michigan: Eastern Michigan University, 2007

Brackey, Jolene. *Creating Moments of Joy: A Journal for Caregivers, Fourth Edition*. West Lafayette, Indiana: Purdue University Press, 2008

Calo-yo, Starr. *Caregiving Tips A-Z: Alzheimer's & Other Dementias*. Orchard Publications, 2008

Coste, Joanne Koenig. *Learning to Speak Alzheimer's: A Groundbreaking Approach for Everyone Dealing with the Disease*. Mariner Books, 2004

Dunn, Hank. *Hard Choices for Loving People: CPR, Artificial Feeding, Comfort Care, and the Patient with a Life-Threatening Illness, Fifth Ed.* A & A Publishers, 2009

Feil, Naomi. *The Validation Breakthrough: Simple Techniques for Communicating with People with 'Alzheimer's-Type Dementia'*. Baltimore, Maryland: Health Professions Press, 2002

Fortanasce, Vincent. *The Anti-Alzheimer's Prescription: The Science-Proven Plan to Start at Any Age*. New York: Gotham, 2009

Genova, Lisa. *Still Alice*. New York, New York: Pocket Books, 2010

Greenblat, Cathy Stein. *Alive with Alzheimer's*. Chicago: University Of Chicago Press, 2004

Ingram, Shannon. *The Heart Way: A Journey from Corporate to Care.* Costa Mesa, CA: Orren Stewart Press, 2005

Mace, Nancy L and Peter V. Rabins. *The 36-Hour Day: A Family Guide to Caring for People with Alzheimer Disease, Other Dementias, and Memory Loss in Later Life,* 4th Edition. Baltimore, Maryland: The Johns Hopkins University Press, 2006

Meyer, Charles. *Surviving Death: A Practical Guide to Caring for the Dying & Bereaved.* New London, Connecticut: Twenty-Third Publications, 1991

Oxford University Press. *Hospice Care for Children.* 2008

Richards, Tom. *An Alzheimer's Surprise Party: Unveiling the Mystery, Inner Experience, and Gifts of Dementia.* Interactive Media, 2009

Schaefer, Dan. *How Do We Tell the Children?* A Step-by-Step Guide for Helping Children Cope When Someone Dies. New York, New York: Newmarket Press, 2002

Shriver, Maria. *What's Happening to Grandpa?* New York, New York: Little, Brown Books for Young Readers, 2004

Smith, Patricia B. *Alzheimer's for Dummies.* New York: John Wiley & Sons, 2003

Strauss, Claudia J. *Talking to Alzheimer's: Simple Ways to Connect When You Visit with a Family Member or Friend.* Oakland, California: New Harbinger Publications, 2002

Twichell, Karen. *A Caregiver's Journey: Finding Your Way.* Indiana: IUniverse, 2002

Wexler, Nancy. *Mama Can't Remember Anymore: Care Management of Aging Parents and Loved Ones.* Wein & Wein Publishers, 1996

We hope you enjoyed this book from AJC Press.

If you would like to receive more information about AJC Press and our products, please contact:

AJC Press

6400 Oak Canyon

Suite 200

Irvine, CA 92618

Email: info@ajcpress.com

www.AJCPRESS.com

All net proceeds from the sale of
The Silverado Story will fund a scholarship
for those dedicating their careers to the
memory-impaired, administered by the
non-profit Silverado Foundation.
For more information, please visit
www.SilveradoSenior.com/Silverado_Foundation.